FEMALE KUNDALINI

MARGARET MIRANDA DEMPSEY

Life Force Books

A Life Force Books Publication

Disclaimer: The information in this book is for educational purposes only and is not intended as medical advice. Neither the author nor the publisher of this work will be held accountable for any use or misuse of the information contained in this book. The author, the publisher, and/or the distributors of this book are not responsible for any effects or consequences from the use of any suggestions, recommendations, or procedures described hereafter.

The author made all reasonable efforts to contact all literature sources quoted in the text.

Life Force Books
PO Box 302
Bayside, CA 95524
www.lifeforcebooks.com

ISBN: 978-0-9896540-1-2

Cover Painting, Pablo Picasso. Cover design by Jessey Clark, Communication Design Associates, CSU - Chico, CA

FEMALE KUNDALINI

"Why be Special...When You Can Be Yourself?"
~ Mooji

ACKNOWLEDGEMENTS

I would like to acknowledge all the people who are too many to mention for making the publication of this book possible. I want to acknowledge my editor and publisher, JJ Semple, who has pushed me to be as honest and authentic as I can possibly be. My last and deepest thanks, however, is given to the powerful, transformative energy that rests at the base of all our spines. It is to this energy that I go on my knees, humble and grateful that I have been able to experience it in one lifetime.

CONTENTS

PART II: REFLECTIONS ON THE JOURNEY

PREFACE

The inner event that awakens Kundalini remains a mystery. In Margaret Dempsey's case, years of Buddhist meditation, galvanized by a traumatic contact with an attractive man, triggered the "uprising of Shakti." Her honesty in not attempting to glamorize the awakening attests to its authenticity. The author's real Self, to which Kundalini eventually brought her, is in evidence from page one, as she describes her upbringing in Catholic Ireland, her days in a boarding school run by nuns, her training as a nurse, and her escape to London, New York and India.

Kundalini is nourished by sexual energy. The fundamental polarity of male and female is at the heart of the cosmos. The polarity of male, Siva, and female, Shakti, is also manifested in the human body, in the sympathetic and parasympathetic nervous systems, and the left and right sides of the brain, a subject on which Margaret Dempsey speaks with great insight.

The polarity is also revealed in her life story. Her father's favouring her over her mother, a young priest recovering from a nervous breakdown who speaks to the hearts of the teenage girls in his congregation, her meeting with Mooji, and the "gorgeous" man who rejected her, are a potent male presence, round which the author's spiritualized womanhood dances. There is a marvellous moment when she speaks of surrender: "I had no idea what I was letting go of... I couldn't have surrendered to nothingness. Somehow I knew there was something to surrender to."

In Tantra, the male god, Siva is both the "Destroyer" (of illusion and ego) and the "Immovable Stillness" of transcendence. The goddess, Shakti, is the energy of creation and manifestation. Kundalini is Shakti's presence in the human body. The book's title, *Female Kundalini*, is therefore apt, not just because it is the document of one woman's Kundalini experience, but because Kundalini Herself, is fundamentally female, even in men.

~ Paul Lyons, London, 2014 – author of *Natalie*

INTRODUCTION

Is female Kundalini different than male Kundalini? Are female bodies different than male bodies? Are feminine egos different than their male counterparts? Kundalini is a biological process with metaphysical ramifications. It is reasonable to infer that a female's way of manifesting Kundalini effects might be somewhat different than a male's.

The first part of this book contains the author's life story. A male child might have made the same life decisions, explored the spiritual path, and chosen the same career paths. Would his awakening have been the same? Probably not. Since Kundalini is *experienced* in so many different ways, both its triggers and its effects vary from subject to subject, irrespective of sex. Not only do character attributes and genetic traits influence the outcome, heredity and environment, education and belief also play a role. All we can do is follow the author's path, noting the many challenges she faced, and ultimately overcame. And, as with most people who activate Kundalini, there were many.

At first, the author was influenced by mostly male interpretations concerning the actuality of her Kundalini experiences. For example, after her second meditation retreat, she was persuaded that the experience had been triggered by drugs, even though we see it wasn't:

"... the experience you had on that retreat was caused by the drugs you had taken two weeks earlier." I just looked at him speechless, and not understanding what I was hearing.

"You haven't taken drugs since then, have you?" he continued.

"No" I replied.

"And you've had no more experiences like that?"

"No" I replied again.

He then told me that the change of environment, food, and intense meditation that a retreat provides meant that the extreme conditions again activated whatever was left of the drug in my brain.

A number of Kundalini-awakened male friends have told me no individual could have persuaded them that their experience might have been induced by a cause other than the one to which they attributed it. This sounds like male braggadocio. In the early stages of my transformational energy experience, I was frequently confused by the advice of seemingly all-knowing third parties.

Yet, are women more malleable when it comes to accepting the so-called "expertise" of the opposite sex? Do they bow to male assumptions merely because they've lived in a male-dominated world for such a long time? I'm not sure, but I do wonder why Dempsey vacillated in this instance, and why she accepted conclusions about the activity and sensations (effects and the triggers) she had observed in the laboratory of her body from individuals who had never experienced Kundalini.

Another challenge women face is parental expectations. Why are these important? They play a large part in the formation of the ego and, therefore, the approach taken to purge the negative effects of the ego after a Kundalini awakening occurs.

I won't go into these differences between the sexes. If you're a member of the fair sex, look at your brother, boyfriend, or father. How are their egos different than yours? How are they brought up to *see* the world, to overcome obstacles, to make their own way in the world? How have their expectations been shaped? How is their sexuality different?

If you believe, as I do,[1] that sexual sublimation is present in all types of Kundalini awakenings — male or female, no matter by what means it is triggered — it follows that the only difference in the sublimation process is that the male anatomy produces seminal fluid while the female anatomy produces cervical fluid. Each, in its turn, is distilled into a powerful *prana* elixir that is then channeled up to the brain.

In my experience, this is a minor issue: whether semen or cervical fluid, it doesn't seem to affect the outcome. What may affect outcome is the manner in which the child's — boy or girl — ego is formed. Nevertheless, the gap between a boy's versus a girl's perspective of, and opportunities in, the world is narrowing. Victorian girls lived in more narrowly defined circumstances. Today, because of all the avenues open to women, parental influence on female progeny is waning.

At the close of World War II, this was not true. For example, 60 years ago, the perspective of Japanese women changed dramatically as General Douglas MacArthur's program of democratization was implemented:

"The General, like Franklin Roosevelt and Adlai Stevenson, was an aristocrat who believed in *noblesse oblige*. He was jealous of his prerogatives and implacable toward those of his own class who pitted themselves against him. But he believed that rank had responsibilities as well as privileges. A fighting commander exposed himself to enemy fire in front of his troops. A general did not allow officers to drink Scotch when the men had only beer. And a gentleman did not look upon women as inferiors. To do so was, by definition, ungentlemanly. It was more; it was, he told those who disagreed with him, sacrilegious. Women, like men, had souls. Therefore, they should be treated equally.

---

1 See *Deciphering the Golden Flower One Secret at a Time* – JJ Semple, Life Force Books, 2007.

"In Japan, they had never been equal. Concubinage and family contract marriages, consigning wives to servility, had been lawful. Women had been forbidden to own property; indeed, they had no economic, legal, or political rights at all. Girls had gone to their own schools, if there were any, after the sixth grade. Public-school courses had been segregated by sex—with the curriculum and texts pitched lower for girls—and there had been no colleges for women. Adultery had been licit for husbands, but illicit for wives. The new Diet had to face this form of sexism squarely in an early session. Under the MacArthur constitution, the lawmakers had a choice: either both partners to an adultery were punishable, or neither was. After anguished debate, the legislators invited correspondence from their constituents. In the past, voters had never written the Diet; they had read its edicts, trembled, and obeyed. Now, in the new spirit, a blizzard of mail arrived, and after reading it the delegates abolished adultery as a crime.

"Contract marriage went; so did concubinage. Marriage and divorce statutes were rewritten. High schools became coeducational, and 26 women's universities opened. In the provinces, women were elected to public office in increasing numbers: 23 to the prefectural assemblies, 74 to city councils, and 707 to town assemblies. By the third year of the occupation, a tradition had been established that every national cabinet must include a woman vice-minister, and before MacArthur left Japan, two Diet committees would be chaired by women. Soon 14,000 women were serving in villages as social workers, and in Tokyo—this sent a shock wave through all Asia—there were 2,000 uniformed women police officers. Girls in shorts began to compete with boys on playgrounds; MacArthur, to his great satisfaction, saw them rapping out hits and chasing flies on the sandlot his Cadillac passed daily."[2]

Today, these types of circumstances still exist in many countries around the world, leaving few opportunities for women living under repressive social policies to further their spiritual interests.

---

2   *American Caesar* – William Manchester, Back Bay Books, 2008-05-12. iBooks.

What does the MacArthur type of social and political reform mean for transformational energy activation (Kundalini, and its related processes) and how the two sexes experience it? Namely, education, civil rights, work, and pay equality give women the time and knowledge to explore spirituality, just as they explored sexuality in the '60s. That's what they are doing in the countries where their perspectives are not limited by reactionary social policy.

There's as much female interest in Kundalini as there is male, and, percentage-wise, probably as many successful female awakenings as male. Just as women are successful business, political, and media leaders in enlightened countries so, too, are they leaders in yoga, meditation, Reiki, and other spiritual pursuits.

Still, if there are differences in the ways women and men experience Kundalini in First World countries, it may stem from the differing expectations parents place on sons and daughters. After awakening Kundalini, however, this changes, as mastering the ego becomes a priority. Nevertheless, there are differences between the sexes, but I find this rather a good thing, as we men can learn from women and they can learn from us. Looking at the author's experience, I am loath to detect anything that happened in her spiritual search that couldn't have happened in a man's.

When I first read Margaret Dempsey's book, I fell in love, not only with her relentless dedication to self-truth, but also with her spirit of adventure. In her single-minded focus and her honesty in pursuit of self-actualization, she reminded me of a distaff Siddhartha. A steadfast explorer, she has accomplished much in a short time, investigating and practicing many techniques and methods, not as a sycophant, but as an actualizer, a person who tests everything in the laboratory of her body, while remaining true to her ultimate goals, so aptly described in the pages that follow.

- JJ Semple, Bayside, CA 2014

PART I

JOURNEY TO KUNDALINI

My Daddy Loves Me More

"Give me the child until he is seven and I will show you the man."

~ St. Ignatius of Loyola

D addy loves me more than he loves you," I said. My mother spun around from the cooker with a wooden spoon in her hand and shouted at me, "You little bitch, I had him before you and I'll have him after you."

I was five years old. In that moment, her expression communicated three things to me that would shape me as an adult:

1) She doesn't love me;
2) I'm on my own; and
3) (focusing on the wooden spoon) I'm not safe in the big world.

Assimilating these insights intellectually did not occur until many years later. I don't remember how the incident ended, but do remember feeling separate, as if I was on my own for the first time.

What shaped my view of love thusly?

My mother was pregnant with me before marrying my dad, which in 1960's Catholic Ireland was a big deal. Out of shame, they left the small village in Ireland and moved to London where I was born. My dad wasn't happy and would say hurtful things to my mum. I saw how she cried and was sad when he spoke that way to her. I didn't understand the content, but I understood the impact firsthand. I was Daddy's girl and whatever I wanted I got. He could get so mad with my mum, but then he would see me and his face would soften and he would smile and give me a hug, all the affection he denied my mum. So, in my five-year-old mind I decided that Daddy loved me more than Mummy and I was testing it out. I could never have anticipated the consequences. The moment I blurted it out, I was no longer a child to my mum. I became another woman, a rival, and a threat.

Decisions we make when we are young have power because they are made in the space of nothing — a vacuum of experience. Looking back at the decisions I made in that space of nothing — no past, no present, no time at all — I am left with the strong belief that we create our lives from the decisions we make.

My relationship with my dad deepened and grew; we were very close. I felt safe and secure with him. He never encouraged me to meet someone. In fact, he would always say, "You're better off without a man, Mag." When I spoke with her about why I didn't seem to have any feelings for guys, Mum would often say, "Dad never wanted you to be with anyone; nobody was ever good enough."

I didn't know how different he was when I wasn't at home until one day I was speaking with my teenage niece and she said, "You have no idea what it's like for Nora (my mum) when you come home, Matt (my dad) is like a schoolboy; he's laughing, joking, won't let anyone else come with him to collect you from the bus. It's awful for her."

Shocked I said, "What do you mean?"

"Well," she continued, "he's so different on the day you come home. Normally, he doesn't talk much, but on the day you come home, he is so excited. He's never like that around Nora."

For most of my life, I have felt uneasy around adults, preferring the company of children. I hide it well. Out with adults, I am friendly. Only I feel a knot of anxiety within. An invitation out for a drink or a meal sees me meticulously planning how long I stay before saying goodbye. Going home, I once again feel tremendous relief at being on my own. How different it is when I'm in the company of children, the younger the better. With them, I feel free, happy, and myself. I have a rapport with them. I am very sensitive to the hurtful things said to children and am always horrified when an adult doesn't see the impact such a hurt creates.

My uneasiness with adults continued as I grew up, and I found myself resisting any efforts to put on lipstick or act grown up. When I was a teenager, all my friends were talking about fancying boys, but I never understood what they were talking about. This ignorance or naivety continued well into adulthood. I remember being with a friend once when she was talking about fancying a man at work. I asked her, "What do you mean by *fancy*?"

She looked at me strangely and said, "Surely you know what it is to fancy someone, that feeling you get when you can't wait to be alone with him."

I looked at her blankly and said, "I've never felt that with anyone I've been out with."

She named a couple of guys I had brief flings with and I said, "It just happened that I was with them, but I never felt what you are calling 'fancying' about any of them. You could line them all up against the wall and I wouldn't feel anything different about any of them."

Her eyes wide as saucers, she then asked, "What about sex?"

I said, "What about it?"

She said, "How can you have sex if you don't feel anything?"

I shrugged my shoulders and said, "Most of the time I wasn't there, I was in the supermarket buying bread."

And that is how it was. I was a virgin until I was 30, and I only allowed myself to have sex because I thought there was something I was missing and didn't want to die a virgin. After that, sex for me felt like abuse, yet it wasn't because I was a consenting adult every time. I didn't understand my feelings of being violated. It felt like abuse, and yet it wasn't. I had such a low sex drive as to be almost asexual. When my friends talked to me about needing sex and being irritable because they weren't getting it, I would look at them like they were from another planet. I had no idea what those feelings and drives were like.

This lack of any kind of sexual radar made flirting or intimacy with the opposite sex a virtual non-starter. Friends would say "X fancies you" and I wouldn't see it, never mind coming up with some kind of signal to show I was interested. That type of non-verbal communication, when attraction is present, was missing for me. I viewed every conversation I had with a man as being friendly without ulterior motives. I was the most naïve of the naïve, an innocent mind trapped in an adult body.

And yet this lack of sexual drive enabled me to focus on spirituality. I was largely free to give everything to Buddhism. This wasn't altogether honest, though. I thought I fancied the Sempai who led the group. He was a big reason I turned up for Buddhist meditation and study every Sunday. Each week, I would plan what I would say to him and how we would get together. And every Sunday evening coming home, I would be annoyed and angry at myself that I didn't do or say what I meant to. Then the cycle would begin all over the next day, fantasizing and planning for the next Sunday evening, what I would do and say. It was exhausting; I was obsessed.

A Single Step

"The spiritual journey is all about trusting a force or energy that has your best interests at heart, and then letting go."
~ Author

I don't remember much of the conversation or how it ended. But when the nun told me the best I could hope for was a factory job, taking tins on and off conveyor belts, it felt like a punch in the stomach.

"I wanted to go to university, study psychology," I stammered.

"I know you're not stupid, Margaret, but these results show you functioning at borderline mental handicapped."

A raise of her eyebrows, an impatient wave of the hand, and I was dismissed. My first major personal crisis, at 15 years old, no less.

The nun had called me into her office to give me the results of an intelligence test that might very well influence my future prospects. My self-esteem bottomed out and I was filled with fear. I didn't tell anyone, least of all my parents. It was something I had to deal with alone. After all, going away to boarding school had been my decision.

So how did I get there? Ironically, I made the decision when only 11 years old. Now I seemed to be freefalling backwards. Perhaps, I'd outsmarted myself. I had to find a way of getting back on track, taking control of my life.

Closing my eyes, I drifted back to the nine-year-old girl who had first connected with "something bigger than myself." I had discovered the ability to tune into *that bigger something* in times of distress as a child.

Constantly teased in school for my prominent buckteeth, I was deeply unhappy. Every night I implored God to remove them. One day I was running to school, hands in my pockets, when I slipped on an uneven slab of pavement. Before I could free my hands, I crashed down face first. Onto the concrete popped my two front teeth. My prayers had been answered.

This had a profound effect, my first spiritual experience. From then on, I just knew there was a God. When you have a prayer answered this way, at the age of nine, it has a powerful effect.

I've had moments of doubt and anger, feelings that life has been, if not worse, at least different for me than for my friends. Feelings of being left out and wondering why. Then I think back to the incident when I was nine and all resentment and confusion melts away. The spiritual path is one of elation and despair, constantly recurring, always uncertain. Many years later, the incident still continues to inspire my confidence in that *something greater than myself.*

I was born and brought up in my parents' faith, as a Catholic in London: my mother, always staunch in her faith; my father, a Catholic only out of duty. I don't remember much about my childhood besides the incident cited above. I do recall loving Enid Blyton's books, especially the *Mallory Towers* series that were all about life in boarding school, which I suppose prompted my fascination with boarding school.

I remember having a problem with my right eye, having to wear ugly black National Health Service glasses, which I refused to do. I also remember my mathematics tutor, how I never cooperated with him, despite the fact that my weakness in this subject was identified early on. When my parents realized I wasn't improving, they let him go.

My eleventh birthday was significant. A friend of my parents gave me a birthday present. "Happy Birthday, Margaret," said Betty, handing over a brightly wrapped package.

"Thanks," I said. I tore off the wrapping and read the title out loud: "A Book of Fortune Telling."

My mother who had watched from the other room came storming in, red faced and shouting, "Give me that book, that's the work of the devil."

"No" I said, holding the book tightly to my chest.

She turned on Betty, saying, "What's wrong with you — bringing her a book like that?"

Seizing my chance to get away, I ran out of the kitchen to my bedroom to read my fought-for treasure. My mother was horrified and tried to take it from me, but the minute I opened the book I knew it was something I wanted to be a part of. I fought to keep it. It gave me a glimpse into a different world. I didn't know what it was; all I knew was I wanted to be a part of it.

That same year, my paternal grandmother died, leaving the family home in Ireland to my father. My parents decided to move there. The decision was made quickly. I don't remember my brothers and me being asked how we felt, nor do I remember saying goodbye to my friends in London. In those days, children weren't consulted; they were simply not included in the process.

Since we went to Ireland every summer for our holidays, it shouldn't have been a shock. But this event rocked my life — the lack of preparation and not being able to say goodbye to my friends reinforced my feelings about the lack of control over my life. I made a decision to take control. I had no idea what form it might take.

Gradually, I adjusted to my new surroundings. One day, Mum and I were out driving. Two girls were hitching. We stopped to pick them up. They told us they were boarders at the convent school in the next town. I immediately began to pump them on everything the *Mallory Towers* books said about boarding school.

"Do you have lots of midnight feasts? Is it great fun? How often do you get to go downtown?" I asked excitedly.

The taller of the two girls laughed and said, "Yes, we have lots of midnight feasts. It's a great place to go to school."

We dropped the girls off and once home, I found the number of the convent, telephoned, and asked to speak to the head of the boarders. Sister Muriel took the call. I explained that I wanted to go to boarding school and asked her if she had a place. Understandably, she was confused, but said *yes*, then asked to speak with my mother. I burst into the kitchen all excited, explained I had Sister Muriel on the phone and they had a place for me in boarding school. I begged to be allowed to go. Mum dried her hands and picked up the phone. I skipped outside to Dad who was working on his vegetable garden. I told him I wanted to go to boarding school.

He looked at me and said, "Is it really what you want?"

"Yes," I said.

"Okay."

And that was that. At the age of 12 I went into an all-girls Catholic boarding school, straight into second year, a situation I came to regret, for the others had already made friends.

ON BEING ALONE

"Confusion is there for a reason. In certainty, there is no growth."

~ Author

Perhaps my reason for going to boarding school was to feel safe and I justified it by saying that it was because of the *Mallory Towers* books and midnight feasts which Enid Blyton wrote about.

Or was the truth that I couldn't face not feeling safe around my mother and I wanted to get away from her? Maybe I saw myself as a source of tension between my parents and believed they would be happier if I wasn't at home. I honestly don't know. I don't remember any closeness with my mother for many years. She made food when I was away in boarding school and always cared for me when I came home, but I had this nagging unease and anxiety whenever I was around her.

The first two years at boarding school weren't easy. I didn't start at the same time as everyone else. This marked me as different from the beginning. I had an English accent to boot. I was unaware of the history taught in the National Schools they called Primary Schools. I didn't know about the English oppression and their taking over certain parts of Ireland.

One day I went to the refectory, to a group of boarders sitting at a table. I hadn't been at the school long so I walked up to them and said hello.

They giggled and looked at each other.

"I'm a boarder here, too," I said, hoping to be invited to sit down.

At first, they just stared at me. Finally, Audrey said, "Why don't you go back to England where you belong."

I stood there for moment, fighting back tears. Then I ran out of the refectory, the words, "We don't want you here!" ringing in my ears.

Being ignored meant I wasn't included in the midnight feasts, which was comical in a tragic way, given that it was my main reason for choosing to go to boarding school. Hearing the laughing and the telltale rustling of forbidden food a couple of cubicles away underscored the extent of my isolation. As a defensive measure, I began to shun company.

Years later, one of these girls said to me, "I can't believe how we hated you when you came here...because of your English accent." When she said that, all the years of hurt disappeared.

It was a Catholic convent so Mass and Benediction and religious matters filled many hours. To cope with my isolation and lack of friends, I tried to decipher the meaning of words in the hymns. I spent hours figuring out what *lose yourself in me* meant from the hymn of the same name; who the "me" was, what it meant to "lose yourself." I spent hours and days alone. I can remember sitting in my cubicle gazing out the window, pondering these things. I never got any answers, but I received great comfort from doing it.

I felt the decision to leave home meant I was on my own; I would no longer be able to confide in my parents. I couldn't tell them how miserable and lonely I was during the first two years. Yet I was grateful to them for respecting my choice. In the years that followed, when first-year students cried on my shoulder about how their parents had "sent them away," I could never say that. Going away was my decision. I had made my bed and had to lie on it.

Mathematics continued to be a problem. At the beginning of each chapter, I would concentrate. The first and second set of exercises went quite well. Then came a complicated third set and I would become totally lost. Every chapter was the same — a promising beginning, only to end up frustrated and bewildered. Something was wrong, but I didn't know what.

Boarders were required to go to Mass every morning. One nun took it upon herself to make sure that I was up in time. Each day this enormous figure in black came into my cubicle and towered over me.

"Get out of that bed, Miss Dempsey; get out on the floor for Mass."

A hand would emerge from the folds of her habit, gather up my duvet, and fling it to the floor. She wouldn't leave until I was out of bed, standing on the cold floor. Then, with a triumphant shake of her head, she would pry her frame through the narrow doorway and disappear. Bleary eyed, I'd get myself ready to go to chapel with the other boarders.

Morning Mass was a humdrum affair. The local priest was the celebrant. We spent our time looking for the sleepiest nuns. I always made it just in time, dreamed my way through it, thinking about breakfast. The chapel was set up with the nuns on one side and the boarders on the other so each could watch the other. The only excitement at Mass was deciding which nun had the most coiffured patch of hair showing outside her veil, proof positive she was fancying the priest. Another giveaway was the coy way they would receive communion. Although they were supposed to be self-effacing — depending on the nun — their actions bordered on the flirtatious.

Sister Josephine was the worst. The way she sashayed up and down the chapel, her skirts swinging from side to side, she must have thought she was on a catwalk. The smiles some of the nuns gave the priest while saying the "Amen," which all Catholics say in response to "Body of Christ" as the priest offers the communion host, might have only been one word, but the eyes of the nuns said far more. They might have been married to God, but God came in a poor second when pitted against a live flesh and blood rival. We were able to watch this because we only lined up for communion after the nuns had finished receiving theirs.

At breakfast, we laughed about it.

"Did you see the way Josephine looked at Father Freddie while he was giving her communion. It's so obvious she fancies him."

"Ha-ha, no" Sarah chimed in. "It's Sister Mary who fancies him. Did you see how blond her hair was outside the veil? I bet she dyed it."

It was a great source of amusement. Although we laughed, I was curious about these women. Why had they chosen to shut themselves away with a bunch of other women, given their obvious interest in the opposite sex?

I continued to read every night. Mills and Boon books were plentiful and I devoured them greedily. When the main light was switched off in the dormitory, my twilight world of book and torch under the duvet began and it would last until the early hours of the morning.

One night I didn't have anything to read, so I went down to the cubicle of a girl who I knew read loads of books. I knocked on her door.

"Come in," she said

When she saw who it was, she said, "What do you want?"

Intimidated because she was older, I stood my ground, my desire to have a book greater than the fear and intimidation I felt.

"Do you have anything to read?" I asked.

She replied, "I have this book, but it's a dirty book and if you get caught with it, it's not mine, okay?"

Eagerly, I agreed and she went to her cupboard and handed me the book. It was entitled *Honey*. Delighted, I thanked her and returned to my cubicle.

I know I read the book completely, but I don't remember it being anything more than another book I read. When I finished it, I put it at the back of my cupboard and promptly forgot about it.

A couple of months later, Elizabeth, who was two years younger than I, asked me if I had anything to read. I remembered *Honey* and ironically demanded she take exactly the same pledge Mary had required of me. Grateful and thankful, she took the book and went away.

A couple of weeks later Elizabeth came to me and said, "Sister Josephine has your book; I'm so sorry."

I felt this sickening thud in the pit of my stomach and said, "How did she get it?"

She said, "We were reading parts of it out loud at the end of the class and she came in and caught us. Now she's asking everyone where it came from."

Fighting down the panic, I said, "That's okay; you don't know where it came from."

She nodded in agreement and went away.

I went back to class, but I couldn't shake an overwhelming feeling of dread. I didn't say anything to anybody.

The next day Elizabeth sought me out in the refectory at lunch and said, "Josephine knows it's your book." I was surprised at how calm I was. I asked "how" and she said, "Anita told her. I am so sorry."

I said, "Don't worry; it's okay."

I couldn't eat anything at lunch and went back to my afternoon class and waited…

The words of the song "Sunrise, this is the last day that I'll ever see, up in that office they're waiting for me, but I go to my Lord with no fear" kept playing round and round in my head. In this hour of desperation, I was once again turning to that "something bigger."

The inner wall of my classroom was a corridor with frosted glass. You could see everyone who walked up and down the corridor although you couldn't distinguish individuals. All you could see were their silhouettes.

I was watching the corridor intently when suddenly I saw a sweep of black pass by the frosted glass. I froze. My mouth went dry. This was it.

The door to the classroom opened and in walked Sister Josephine, her mouth set in a thin tight line. She said something to the nun teaching who gave me a shocked open-mouthed stare.

Sister Josephine came to my desk and said, "Out." She turned on her heel and strode out. I stood up and followed her. We proceeded to make the long walk from my classroom to her office without talking. She broke the silence by saying, "Do you have any idea why I have taken you out of class"

"No," I replied.

"Oh come on, Margaret," she said." I don't take you out of class for nothing."

I gave in and said, "Is it about a book?"

Triumphantly, she nodded her head. She had her confession just as she wanted. We continued the rest of the interminable journey in silence.

When I got into her office, I saw that we weren't alone. The head of the boarders was there, as was the career guidance teacher. A teacher, Mr. Watson, was also there, but I didn't understand why.

The offending book was on the table in all its glory. To my surprise, it had pages turned down and parts underlined.

"Is this your book?" asked Sister Josephine as she waved it at me.

"No, Sister," I replied

"Whose book is it then?"

"I got it from a daygirl, I lied."

That seemed to take the wind out of her because she said, "Well, as it came in from a daygirl, it will be up to Sister Muriel as head of the boarders to deal with the effect of your bringing it into the boarding school." I can't remember much of what else was said.

Then Sister Muriel said, "Come with me."

We left and outside she said, "I am going to have to tell your parents about this. Now go back to class."

Dumbfounded, I looked up at her. I couldn't for the life of me understand what the big deal was.

She left me standing bewildered and alone. I went back to class. A couple of evenings later, I was in study hall when a note was passed to me from one of the other boarders. It read, "Your mum and dad are here; they're getting out of the car."

I stood up to see our blue Hillman Hunter car sitting stationary under the street light and my mum and dad going up the steps of the boarding school with Sister Muriel standing at the top of the stairs waiting. To do what...I honestly didn't know.

Feeling really sick, I tried to study, but once again just waited.

Thirty minutes later the study door opened and Sister Muriel came in and said something to the nun supervising study and then made her way over to me.

She said, "Come outside." I stood up and meekly followed her.

She said, "Your parents are here."

I said to her, "What did you want to gain from bringing them up?"

She said, "It's not acceptable for a book like that to be brought into the boarding school. They are waiting for you." I began to cry.

We walked to the room where my parents were waiting. The moment I saw my dad, I ran over and burst into tears. He just looked at me and held me. My mother's face said it all, such disapproval and distance.

She asked, "Is this true?"

Through my pain, I wanted to blurt out, "What do you bloody think?" But I didn't.

I just nodded and she said, "We are so disappointed in you," which was greeted by more of my tears.

Sister Muriel then relented and said she thought I had learned a lesson, it would never happen again, and she said the incident was now closed.

I wish it had been closed for my mother. For months afterwards, every time I went home, each book I had with me was censured and I was regularly reminded of the shame I had brought on the family.

One morning there was a different priest saying Mass. It was rumored this priest had had a nervous breakdown and had just returned to his parish duties. As an introduction back into the community, he had already given a sermon on the beauty of sex at the local old folks' home. The daygirls told the boarders about it; it was the only thing anyone in the town was talking about. Ground-breaking stuff — a priest giving a sermon on sex in any situation, let alone in an old folks' home. And then to promote it was unheard of! On the morning he came to say

Mass, the boarders were waiting for him gleefully. I was up and dressed before my daily "alarm clock" in the shape of a nun arrived. I sprang out of bed with a delicious sense of anticipation, dressed quickly, and hurried to the chapel for Mass.

Young and affable, he only said Mass once, but two things he said have stayed with me:

"You girls, every morning you say, *Good God, it's morning!* Why don't you say *Good morning, God?*"

I don't know if it was the rhythm of the sentence or an early morning buzz, but it resonated with me. For years, I have said this the minute I wake up, gazing out the window as I say *Good morning, God.* This practice allows me to wake up every morning, looking forward to, rather than dreading, the day. I feel contentment rising from within. It allows me to ignore the usual everyday worries, until I have connected with that sense of space I call *Presence,* which for me, represents the gift of another day. It is always joyous, no matter what concerns my mind has to process afterwards. I wake up with joyful anticipation. I'm sure this practice, done continuously for many years, allows me to be this way.

Through the years, my practice has laid down a neural pathway in the brain. From the routine I follow every morning when I wake up and every night before I go to sleep, actual neural pathways have been created. Maintaining them is imperative. If not repeated, the pathway doesn't get the necessary reinforcement and simply fades away.

With the increased use of magnetic resonance imaging (MRI), neuroscientists are finding out more about neural pathways. In the past, little was known about how the brain functioned and even less about how metaphysical phenomena might be attributed to the brain, or even exist beyond our bodies. To illustrate the power of constant mindfulness and its ability to lay down and deepen neural pathways, an ancient Indian story comes to mind.

There were two Indian men who knew each other. At 6:00 PM every evening one of the men lit his candle and incense and did his *puja* — a Hindu devotional practice. The other man did not. They both died and met in Heaven.

The man who lit his candle each evening was angry and said to God, "Why is this man here? I know that he never lit a candle any evening or did *puja*."

God replied: "What you don't know is that I was his first thought in the morning and his last thought at night. For you, I was only a thought at six PM, and only then for fifteen minutes."

When I heard this story, I understood why continuous remembering is important for spiritual development. It is not a journey to be taken with the attitude of *I will fit it in when I can*. Continuous mindfulness brings about a profound shift in consciousness without which Enlightenment cannot take place. To quote an unnamed Sufi poet:

I thought of YOU so often that I completely became YOU.
Little by little YOU drew closer.
And slowly but surely I passed away.

The importance of constant mindfulness came from a statement by a priest during my teens. Later, I found it echoed by the words of Sufi poets and Indian sages. To experience the state of mind that is free from suffering, which is the ultimate achievement for all Beings, is not a goal that can be achieved overnight. It is a life-long journey. Sometimes many lifetimes, which only start in earnest when we say *yes* to that *call that comes in many forms*.

The second thing that priest said resulted in him never again saying the convent Mass. He said: "God wants spiritual fruit, not religious nuts."

You can imagine how this went down with the nuns. I stole a look at their side of the chapel, watched their faces say it all. Every one of them went rigid with shock. The priest continued his sermon, totally oblivious to the effect his words were having. I couldn't believe what I'd heard. The words ricocheted round my brain – *spiritual, religious, fruit, nut*. I knew this sentence was significant, something for me to understand, even though I wasn't clear about what it meant. Once I absorbed the meaning,

I realized the two were different and I made my choice about which one to pursue —spiritual, not religious. I didn't exactly know how to achieve it. Yet, the notion of being spiritual gripped me in a way that being religious didn't.

Years later, having a drink with Julie, a friend from boarding school, I recall asking her, "Do you remember that strange priest? The one who said Mass only once?"

"No," she replied.

"You don't remember how young he was? Or his sermon: 'God wants spiritual fruit, not religious nuts'; how it set the whole school off?"

"I don't remember very much from school," said Julie.

"I can't believe how something that had such a profound impact on me didn't even register on you."

"The only thing I remember about mass was how much I hated it. Probably made me forget the rest," she said.

"Anyway, it had an impact on me, set me off on the spiritual path," I told her.

For a couple of minutes, we sipped at our drinks and stared out the windows. Neither of us spoke, as if our diverging recollections had cast a fresh light on our relationship.

To my amazement, she had no memory of the priest or what he said. She had to have been there; morning Mass was mandatory. It struck me that an event — so significant and life changing for me — meant so little to my friend. Casual circumstances like this convince me there is a higher purpose to all of our lives. All that is required from us is to remain alert and aware, true to others and ourselves.

Religion prevents people from getting in touch with their underlying spirituality. The emphasis is on rules and rituals, which leaves no energy for anything else. That I had this *sense of the Divine,* and I was aware that I had it, blew me away, especially being so very young. Where did it come from? Deciding a spiritual path would be the hallmark of my life from that point on?

The final three years in school were my happiest. I chose to do TY (Transition Year). So, instead of moving into fifth year, I did an in-between year, starting afresh with girls from different classes, which provided me with a chance to make friends from the beginning. In TY, students don't do the usual subjects, which meant I had a year free of mathematics. Instead, we did drama, media, secretarial skills, and other unconventional subjects. The year also involved different kinds of professional experiences, such as working in a shop, in a primary school, an old folks' home, and in a home for those with learning difficulties.

Participating in these work experiences, I developed empathy for people everywhere I went. Whether with the people in the old folks' home or with the children in the local primary school, I tuned into them easily. My reports from the different places I worked were glowing. I decided that when I completed my final exams, I would study psychology and told my parents about my plans. They were thrilled with my decision and completely supported me.

Back studying for my final exams, mathematics continued to be a problem. How I envied my schoolmates who enjoyed solving problems. Even though I tried to concentrate, whenever we learned something new, I knew that, at some point in the chapter, I would lose my way as the exercises became more difficult. In the end, this was something I accepted. I was very excited about going to university to study psychology because I felt drawn to the subject. But something happened that would prevent me from being an undergraduate in the immediate future.

A couple of months before my final exams, the nun in charge of career guidance came into the classroom, saying she was going to give us some intelligence tests. When I took mine, I set about it with enthusiasm, but didn't manage to complete all the exercises and ran out of time very quickly. I was a bit surprised about this, but didn't dwell on it. The results were due a couple of days later. The nun brought each of us into her office to discuss the results individually. When it was my turn, she said to me in the gravest tone: "Now, Margaret, I know you're not stupid, but according to these results, you are functioning at borderline mental handicap."

As the words spilled out of her mouth, I felt myself reeling, losing control. Looking back at this event, I am amazed at how little fight was in me. It never dawned on me that what the nun had said wasn't true or that she was being spiteful; it's just that I was caught so off guard, so utterly unprepared.

Yet, I probed deeper, "I want to go to university," I said. "I want to study psychology."

With a wave of her black arm, she replied, "Oh no, that's never going to be possible for you. The best you can hope for is one of those jobs where you take tins of beans on and off conveyor belts."

The best I could do was a kind of makeshift lateral thinking by which I reasoned that, if I were mentally handicapped, then I would work with mentally handicapped children and adults. It meant not pursuing a university education, that I might never be able to realize my dreams.

I made the decision out of confusion. I reasoned that, if this was my level of mental proficiency, I belonged with these people. The decision, arrived at out of the blue, without speaking to anyone, confused and disappointed my parents. I turned my back on going to university and instead, enrolled to become a Registered Nurse for the Mentally Handicapped (RNMH).

When I told my mum and dad that I was shelving my plans to go to university and was going to train to be a nurse instead, they tried to persuade me to change my mind; but, once they saw that it was made up, they accepted it as they had done so many times in the past.

Trying to Adjust

"Hold fast to nothing."
~ Siddhārtha Gautama, The Buddha

As a child, I had never asked for a nurse's uniform or showed the least bit of interest in nursing. My parents knew this, which was why they were so confused when I changed my mind about my not wanting to study psychology. I couldn't, or wouldn't, tell them the real reason I changed my mind. So I ended up training as a nurse for learning difficulties with the Sisters of La Sagesse in Cregg House, Ireland, for three years (beginning in 1981).

I learned much from working with children and adults. By showing undisguised delight, they taught me how to be unconditionally kind. When I walked into the ward in the morning, they beamed warmth and goodwill. I learned about innocence and the value of simplicity. I also gained insight into my nature.

Cregg House was divided into wards, each with its own name. The Infirmary was the ward for children with profound learning difficulties and housed Sarah, a child born with hydrocephalus, a condition where a baby is born with a huge head and a tiny body. She was 11 years old, deaf and blind, and incredibly sensitive to pain. In order to dress her, I had to pull down the sides of the cot and move her head. The fear she felt when the cot was being moved caused her to freeze up. Tears came into her eyes because she knew the pain that would soon follow. It broke my heart. Every time I had to dress her, I felt her distress. I found that by gently rubbing her face before taking down the sides of the cot, she relaxed a little, so I always did this before dressing her. She never had any visitors. I used to wonder why nobody came to see her. What sort of mother did she have, who never came to visit? The more time I spent with Sarah, the more I realized she was more than the sum total of her illness. I became angrier and angrier that she was so alone in the world. I spent a significant amount of time building up a picture of her cold, hard, unfeeling parents. I became quite bitter towards them, harboring thoughts like *this child didn't ask to be born.* Each time I thought about her, a well of righteous indignation rose up within me.

Being sent out on secondments (the detachment of a person from their regular organization for temporary assignment elsewhere) was part of a registered nurse's training. For me, it was one week to the general hospital, the next to the psychiatric hospital.

In the general hospital one day, I was waiting for the lift to an upper floor. It arrived and the doors opened. Inside was a porter. I walked in and the doors closed. He saw my badge.

"Ah! You're out from Cregg House," he said.

"Yes," I replied

"I have a daughter out there," he said.

Images of all the children flashed through my mind — who could it be? Before I could say anything, he answered the question I was grappling with.

"It's Sarah in the Infirmary," he said, and my heart almost stopped.

Here I was, face-to-face with the "cold unfeeling person," a picture of whom I had built up in my mind. And yet he seemed to be nothing like the vision I had concocted.

"I suppose you think I'm terrible for never going out to visit her," he said.

I had nursed resentment towards this man for so long, I had to say something to justify my judgment of him.

"I think you're denying the child a basic right," I said.

He sighed and looked sad. "How long have you been out there?" he asked.

"This is my second year," I replied.

"Up to three years ago, my wife and I went out every Sunday to visit Sarah. For the rest of the week, my wife would be so upset it affected our three other children. Finally, we made a decision for the sake of the whole family. Sarah was in good hands with the nurses at Cregg House and by not going to see her, we could move on with our lives."

I felt myself go hot and cold as he was speaking, ashamed that I had judged this man without knowing the circumstances. I was so caught up with wanting to be right in my opinion of Sarah's parents, that they were cold and unfeeling. This entrenched position did not allow any space for empathy. I realized that we would never see the total picture, so making a judgment on a small piece of information, no matter how convincing, is misguided.

When we cling to strongly-held views and they become the truth rather than simply a view or an opinion, there is no room for anything else. I saw how limiting holding onto any view is. The Buddha said, "Hold fast to nothing." He meant: Don't hold any fixed and permanent ideas about anything in life; everything is impermanent and changing.

In that brief encounter with a stranger in a lift, I was given a spiritual lesson – the importance of empathy and being non-judgmental, essential qualities for the spiritual path.

As the nurse training progressed, I knew this vocation wasn't for me. I started making mistakes and getting stressed. Working with the mildly affected patients was easier and more enjoyable than working with the profoundly disturbed ones. I became close to a teenage boy with mild cerebral palsy.

One day we were in the ward when he asked, "Why do people look at me funny when I say that I'm from Cregg House?"

Startled, I looked into his eyes and said, "Cregg is filled with special people. That's why they look at you funny because they see how special you are."

My heart ached for him because, maybe like me, he knew there was something different about him, but didn't understand what.

Because I was not cut out to be a nurse, there were many mishaps while I was training. Once, a boy was brought to the doctor because he couldn't sleep at night. The doctor prescribed 2.5 mls of a tranquilizer. I was on night duty. I misread the dosage and ended up giving the boy 12.5 mls. When I discovered my mistake, I was distraught, but didn't tell anybody. I was ashamed and afraid of the consequences. The other nurses couldn't believe it when he didn't wake up until almost 9:00 AM the next morning. I kept a vigil by his bedside, willing him to wake up. Nobody was happier than I when he finally emerged from sleep.

This kind of incident took its toll on me. I developed a tremor in my hand from stress. A doctor prescribed tranquilizers, which I never took.

In the course of my training, I came into contact with psychology once again and had no problem understanding the theory. Indeed, I absolutely loved it. I resolved that when I finished my training, I would do what I'd always wanted, which was to study psychology. I talked it over with my parents and they were delighted that I was going to university, even if was later than they had initially hoped.

I often think back on those years spent at Cregg House, and ask myself: *Why was I there, what was the purpose of it?* Three tough years I didn't enjoy.

Perhaps if I'd gone straight to university, I wouldn't have learned the value of empathy I got from working with people with learning difficulties. To accept the human condition, the spiritual path demands empathy. It also requires wisdom. Wisdom without empathy is a sterile condition. Yet, empathy devoid of wisdom is simply a way of being foolish. To be a fully-rounded person, it's important to balance wisdom with empathy. The time spent with these innocent souls made me more empathetic and wiser.

BACK ON TRACK

"The soul has its own language, different from the language of the mind."

~ Author

Once my final nursing examinations were over, I enrolled in psychology at an Irish university. Because of my long-standing weakness in mathematics, I loved every subject except statistics. Although I worked hard, the comments of the nun still rang in my ears. I always felt failure was just around the corner.

Only the top 20 students would get through to Years Two and Three, and there were 350 of us trying to qualify. My hard work paid off and I came in at the top of the class my first year. This boosted my confidence and went a long way to purging the demons that had haunted me since boarding school.

It was through studying psychology that I was given a reason for feeling so different. To quantify this difference is difficult. It was a feeling of not being understood, not belonging, of seeing things differently than everyone else. I was more sensitive and felt things more. From a young age, when I walked into a room I would know immediately who felt at ease and who felt uncomfortable. It was something I picked up on, an intuitive mechanism I had. When someone spoke to me, I had to wait until they finished each sentence so I could make a picture. I would then respond based on the picture I had constructed. I still continue to communicate this way; it's made me a good listener!

One day our lecturer in cognitive psychology told us that she was going to speak about the brain. She explained that it is divided into right and left hemispheres or sides. In general, what we see through the right eye affects the left side of the brain and vice versa. She had my attention; I straightened up from my slouching posture. She said the right and the left sides are held together by fibers that enable the two parts of the brain to communicate with each other.

She spoke about several brain studies in the 1960s. The fibers holding the two parts were cut to treat patients with a particular form of epilepsy. Without the fibers to enable communication between the left and right sides, they discovered that each side performed different functions. The left brain is analytical and logical. The right brain is sensitive and intuitive. The left brain thinks in words, the right in pictures. The left brain operates sequentially, working with each part to get to the whole; the right sees the whole first and then works backwards. As she was delivering this information, my world was rocking. Everything she said about right brain functioning had my whole being crying, "Yes, that's me!" When she finished the lecture, I sat in my seat stunned, but relieved. I wasn't weird or stupid; I was simply right-brained. This was why I couldn't do math because it is a step-by-step activity, always building on what has gone before. *Eureka*!

I saw my life and how I had always made spur-of-the-moment decisions without working out the specific steps. I noticed many of my friends thought and planned meticulously before doing anything. I would just act and then deal with the consequences. I thought of the flash decision I made to go to boarding school, and the one to train as a nurse. These were immediate decisions, made without any hesitation or forethought.

This type of organizing is a pattern throughout my life. Sometimes it doesn't work in my favor (the choice I made to go to nursing school, for instance). But, are they not inevitable given my right brain dominance, an intellectual process without the moderating influence of the left brain? With reduced activity in the left brain, the fibers connecting both sides don't pass enough information to the right side, leaving it free to operate unfettered.

Remembering what the lecturer had said about the connection between the eye and the brain, I realized my problems were connected with my lazy right eye, so I formed the following hypothesis:

"If only a limited amount of visual information travelled to the left side of the brain through my lazy right eye (a condition I'd had since childhood), it made sense that I would be bad at mathematics because math is analytical and logical."

The left brain — used for more complicated, analytical activities — was not being stimulated. Perhaps this explained my inability at mathematics. I could barely do simple addition and subtraction; more complicated operations were impossible. In hindsight, I was grasping at straws.

Although I qualified with a 2:1 BA degree, I had no idea what to do with my life. Counting nursing and university, I had studied for six years. A BA on its own is relatively useless so unless I was prepared to do a Masters degree, it was unlikely that I would get a job as a psychologist.

I was tired of studying and I wanted to earn money. I had worked in a bookshop in New York the summer before (on a student work visa) and while there had met an elderly man for whom my friend worked. She didn't like him, called him "the reptile." Why she called him this I don't know and I never asked. She invited me to meet him one evening and I liked him immediately. When I returned to Ireland after the summer, she called and told me that she had quit her job, telling me that Mr. J was too demanding and fussy. Later that year, I finished my degree and wrote to him, explaining that I would love to return to New York and work for him after finishing my degree, if he could offer me a job. He wrote back explaining that he did have a job opening as one of the women who worked for him was leaving to get married.

And, so it was that I became his nursing assistant. Mr. J lived on Park Avenue where I found a style of living and an exposure to wealth on a scale I had never seen before. His apartment was full of Henry Moore sculptures and Miro paintings, marble bathrooms — in short, the very best of everything. He was a taxation lawyer who had lost his wife after 53 years of marriage; he had no children. Each week he had special carnations flown in, and would wear one in his lapel every day.

My living quarters were on the ground floor. I occupied a tasteful studio flat with a television, video, and phone. In addition to me, he employed a French housekeeper who lived upstairs in the apartment. I would go upstairs at 8:00 AM to prepare the pills he took with his breakfast and take the tray into the room where he sat reading the paper and listening to whatever was going on at the stock exchange. He was always friendly and said, "Good morning. Did you sleep alright, dear?"

"Yes, thank you," I would always answer.

He had a bell at the side of his chair that he would ring when he had finished his breakfast and wanted his tray to be collected. Then he would shower and get ready to go to work. He would appear in the kitchen. Annette would take a carnation out of the fridge and attach it to his jacket. Then the intercom would announce that his chauffeur was waiting and, with a smile and a wave, he would leave for the day.

My job was then to clean the kitchen and bathrooms while Annette made a list of things that were needed. He was a strict Jew so everything had to be kosher. I had from 11:00 AM to 3:00 PM off. I would wander down Madison and Lexington Avenues. Even though these areas of New York are not poor, I always felt the contrast between what I left behind in his Park Avenue apartment and what I saw on the streets. On one particular day, I was struck by the difference between the wealth of my surroundings and a man with one leg holding out a cup, begging me for "any cents."

I wondered why the gap was so great. One afternoon I returned to serve Mr. J his supper, feeling especially uncomfortable. I decided to ask him about this and waited for an opportunity. It came one day as he spoke to the housekeeper and me about putting on a dinner party for some wealthy friends and the special gold-lined plates he wanted to use. This was the last straw.

"How can you live in such wealth when two blocks down, there are people starving?" I blurted out.

There was a shocked silence. He looked at me keenly as though weighing whether or not to answer. Then he sighed and said:

"When I was younger, the only jobs that nobody else wanted were given to Jews, which meant that if I was to be successful I needed to become either a doctor or a lawyer. I chose to be a lawyer and all of the wealth I have, I made myself. Everyone can be wealthy if they work hard enough." With that, he turned away; the subject was closed.

When my visa ran out, I felt uncomfortable about being there illegally. So did Mr. J. He had asked me what I wanted to do with my life, and I said I wanted to do more study. He said if I got accepted at an American university for a Masters program, he would sponsor me. Thrilled, I signed up for the American SAT tests, which are similar to the Intelligence Quotient tests in the UK. The SAT tested my aptitude in English and mathematics and my achievement level in psychology. While my results were in the top 10 percent in psychology, my mathematics results were in the bottom 10 percent. Succeeding in one part didn't compensate for failure in the other. I lost the chance to study for a Masters in New York. I was devastated. So was Mr. J. Reluctantly, we agreed staying in New York illegally was not an option.

What came next surprised me. His expression changed. I had a feeling he was going to propose something big. He looked intently into my eyes and said, "Marry me, dear. I'll be dead in a couple of years and you'll be a very wealthy woman."

I was so shocked at this that I didn't know what to say. I knew he was fond of me because he had started spending an ever-increasing amount of time telling me about his life and the stock market. I had grown fond of him to the point of telling him to be careful, *that people might only like you for your money.*

I will always remember the answer he gave me. "Dear, you don't know how much pleasure it gives me to give, and I am wealthy enough to do so," he said.

To say that I didn't give his proposal any thought would be a lie. For a moment, I seriously considered it. I visualized myself safe and secure in that lovely apartment, not worrying about being different or not belonging — being in this very affluent life and having everything materially that I wanted. Then I saw the face of my dad and knew that he would never understand if I married someone 88 when I was just 25. Come to think of it, not many people would; and, I would probably have been seen as a gold digger who only married him for his money. I didn't love him, so marrying him just for a change of lifestyle would have been wrong. Had I been in love with him, perhaps I would have taken the chance and dealt with the accusations, but I wasn't.

Now, much older and wiser, I often think back on that time and ponder my choice. I have read stories in the papers about younger women marrying older, rich men. In most cases these women are judged as marrying only for money. I am unwilling to judge them because it's quite possible they are marrying for love, in spite of what popular opinion asserts. I turned down the proposal because there was something else I was going after that had nothing to do with money. I wasn't aware of this at the time.

While I was working for Mr. J, I don't remember having the same spiritual curiosity I had in school or during my nursing days. It was a quiet time for me. My awareness of "something bigger" has always been more apparent in times of loneliness and uncertainty.

Intuitively, I knew if I married him it would be for the wrong reasons. When we do things for the wrong reasons, the mind puts forward rationalizations to excuse our behavior, squelching the true inner voice, our guide throughout this human life. Being true to oneself involves listening to the inner voice and acting on it. If something doesn't feel right, it shouldn't be done. When this is applied to the spiritual path, it can be confusing because there are long periods when nothing feels right, a kind of limbo, a place I have often found myself, alone in a dark tunnel.

Those times in the tunnel do end, replaced by greater awareness, peace, and calm. It's almost as if the quiet times are times of consolidation, times when you don't have to *do*, times when hidden forces inside you work silently, beyond the reach of your cognition. Just be ready to listen to the inner voice when it finally awakens. It may come in the form of intuition, or perhaps some other form.

On and off, I wondered why my plans to succeed with psychology always failed. Each time, I felt angry and frustrated with the inadequacy of my left brain. I started talking with friends quite openly about my "left brain" problem. In fact, it became the only subject I talked about. Friends who once listened patiently became increasingly exasperated.

"Oh, for God's sake," said one friend when I interrupted him with my right brain theory. "I wish you would give it a rest. There's nothing wrong with your brain, you just have a mental block about math."

Upset, I said, "It's all right for you, you have a proper functioning brain; you have no idea what it's like for me. I can't do math, so I'm never going to be able to get a good job. I think differently than everyone else, I don't belong. I feel so different, it's scary. I make snap decisions, act impulsively. I don't think things through. I feel like a child in an adult world. But you're right about one thing."

"What's that?" he asked.

"I shouldn't be shooting my mouth off to just anybody. It takes a perceptive person to understand."

I was convinced I was a right-brained woman living in a left-brained world. I didn't know how I was going to survive in such a world. In fact, I didn't think there was a place for me in this world. I knew I had to do something about it, but I didn't know what, so I returned to London, unsure of what my next step would be.

THE REAL WORK BEGINS

"Spiritual awakening happens when consciousness shifts such that the familiar is seen in a different light."

~ Author

B ack in London as I pondered, the urge to do something "spiritual" reemerged from a wellspring where it had been sleeping. I owned tarot cards that I read for relatives. My mother thought that reading the cards was "working with the devil," but she didn't try to stop me from doing it. I never felt confident about giving readings, even though I always got good feedback from those I read to.

One day I visited the College of Psychic Studies in London to check out the available courses. Thumbing through the course syllabus, I saw a course on Cheirology, the ancient art of palm reading. I enrolled for the six-week course that involved reading the lines on the hands according to the Chinese elements of earth, water, fire, and air. This appealed to me more than the traditional way that hands were read — more scientific than intuitive. I pestered my friends to give me their handprints and at the end of the course had quite a formidable collection. I passed the foundation exam at the end. The purpose of the exam was to analyze a set of handprints and the personality that went with those hands.

After the Cheirology course was finished, I had a strong inner urge to ring up Andrew, the guy who had taught the course, and ask him what he was doing next.

He said, "I am starting a beginners' course in Buddhism. Would you be interested?"

Having been born and brought up Catholic, I had never heard of Buddhism, so I asked what it was.

He replied, "Come along to the first class and see what you think. If you don't think it's for you, then you don't have to come anymore."

In the first class held at his home in London, there were five of us sitting on the floor in a room. He talked about Buddhism (Mahayana) being a philosophy and a way to live life, more than a religion. This got my attention. There was something about religion and, in my case, the Catholic religion that unsettled me, something contrary to what I had been taught when I was young. According to Buddhism, said Andrew, there isn't some man in the sky who decides if we are going to be happy or not. It's the way we live our lives (our karma) that determines how content we are. For many years, I had been uneasy with the Catholic idea of a God who rewarded me when I was good and punished me when I was bad. The uneasiness stemmed from my experience of God's answering my prayer when I was nine and taking away the teeth that were causing me such misery.

Andrew spoke about achieving enlightenment and being free from suffering. He explained that the Buddha said that it was possible to become enlightened in one lifetime. I listened closely with a childlike belief, unquestioning and completely open to everything he said. He explained how Buddhism was concerned with developing wisdom and compassion.

Karma was explained as the results of actions undertaken in past lives. The way we live this life determines our future lives. Karma introduces the idea of reincarnation. Cycling back through many lifetimes to learn lessons and have experiences in order to perfect ourselves over time made perfect sense to me. Learning about Buddhism that night gave me the feeling that I had come home. I had found the place where I belonged. Everything about it resonated. I also appreciated that the Buddha encouraged people to try Buddhism, but if they found it wasn't for them, they could look for something else. Compared to the dogma and rigidity of Catholicism, this was a lot more flexible.

I heard one thing that night that altered my consciousness profoundly and resonated in the deepest part of me.

Andrew said, "Central to Mahayana Buddhism is the idea of a Bodhisattva. This is someone who is enlightened, someone who understands the causes of suffering and how to alleviate them, and who chooses to stay in the world until everybody else has become enlightened."

He had just finished the sentence when I was gripped by the most intense desire and the thought *I want to be this.* In that instant, it seemed like time stood still and there was just a burning desire in me that came from nowhere. I didn't know how it would happen; I just knew I wanted it to. I found myself making a silent vow: *may I attain this for the benefit of all human beings*. I also didn't know it, but that moment marked a turning point on my spiritual journey. I gave up the pursuit of individual enlightenment, except to the extent it might benefit all sentient beings in their quest for enlightenment.

The moment passed and the class continued. I hung onto Andrew's every word. At the end of the evening, I told him that I wanted to continue with the course. Over the next 10 weeks, I built up my knowledge and understanding about The Four Noble Truths, The Noble Eightfold Path.

When Andrew explained the first noble truth that everything is suffering, my entire being rebelled, saying, "No, not *everything* is suffering." I refused to accept this, or more accurately, my mind wouldn't accept this because it was negative and depressing. But when I looked closely, I saw through my own experience that life is suffering. I wanted pleasant things to continue and unpleasant things to end.

The second noble truth is that the cause of this suffering is attachment. Instead of accepting everything just the way it is and the way it isn't, we cling onto things that are pleasant and avoid things that are unpleasant. We want things to be different than they are and this wanting, or attachment to the way we want things to be rather than the way they are, is the cause of suffering for human beings.

The third noble truth is that there is a way to free oneself from the cycle of suffering, and the fourth noble truth is that the way to freedom is the eightfold noble pathway.

I could see the logic quite easily of The Four Noble Truths, but when it came to the eight virtues of the path, I felt more conflict. I could never live the kind of life laid down by the eightfold path and didn't try very hard to, either. It was more an intellectual interest rather than an actual plan for life at that time.

I learned about the Sutras (parables) that the Buddha gave to his disciples who then wrote them down. I loved every minute. Hearing the Sutras, I understood them at an intuitive level, but couldn't yet voice their essence.

Andrew was part of a larger Buddhist organization founded by a man in Norwich. I paid the fees for the Buddhist course to this organization, but had not met anyone else connected with the group. I was happy with this arrangement. Andrew also taught Kempo or Chinese Kick Boxing and yoga so I started these.

One evening I was invited to a party to meet the man who had founded the organization. When I met him, I was disappointed. I expected a man who would personify the Buddhist qualities of wisdom and compassion. Instead, I met a man who was rude, obnoxious, and egomaniacal. And yet, the students were in awe of him. This confused me. I put it down to my not knowing enough about how teachers operate, as I had never had one. That week I had been learning about how destructive the ego is to spiritual realization. I thought it was just my ego protesting, so I didn't say anything. I got on well with many people at the party and learned about other classes throughout London. At this point, I had finished my Buddhist beginner's class and was keen to deepen my study and understanding.

One of the girls at the party told me about a weekly Sunday evening meditation group at her house and invited me to join. I agreed without hesitation. For the first time, I was going to meditate. When I started practicing with this group, I encountered a kind of incongruity. On the one hand, I loved Buddhist theory; on the other, I found meditating very difficult.

Each Sunday evening, we would all straggle in at different times, sitting for a while around a table chatting about the week we had. At 7:00 PM, we would go upstairs to the meditation room, and the Sempai who lived in the house would lead the group in meditation.

The session would last for about 45 minutes. During that time, I sat and looked around me, at books on the shelf, at the guitar in the corner, or the trees out the window — doing anything but watching my breath. I looked at the Sempai sitting straight as a ramrod in a kind of trance. I watched the other devotees with their eyes closed, seemingly somewhere I was not able to enter and wondered what it was all about. I tried to meditate. I began in earnest to be aware of my breath, counting in and out as one breath followed another. But then my mind wandered and I thought about everything and anything. However, my real, existential attention was focused on how bored I was and how glad I was when the bell went off to signify the end of meditation so we could all go downstairs for my favorite part of the evening.

Once downstairs, I was always the first to break the silence. I would make some stupid and inane comment that the Sempai would greet with a stony stare. I didn't realize that after a meditation session it takes a while for the mind to return to everyday matters. I hadn't gotten that deep into the meditation so my mind was still as busy and active after as it was before. My immediate prattle interrupted that gradual return for others. We never spoke about what the practitioners experienced during their meditation, although I was dying to ask, but didn't dare.

Then we began the study part of the evening. We were studying a Buddhist text called *Seven Works of Vasubandhu* by Stefan Anacker, and I loved it. Someone would read a paragraph aloud and then we would go through it, line-by-line, analyzing it, trying to understand what it meant. Sometimes the thoughts about the lines and their meaning would come to me very quickly, but then disappear from my mind before I had the chance to share them with the others.

There were times when I would try to explain what was in my mind, but the words didn't come out as accurately as my thoughts. This was frustrating for me and confusing for the others as they tried to understand where I was coming from. But in spite of my shortcomings, I lived for these Sunday evening meetings; nothing could make me cancel them.

I didn't tell many people what I did on a Sunday evening. At one point, I had a boyfriend and told him that I would see him anytime, but not on Sunday evenings. I didn't tell him why. At first this was okay, but eventually he started to quiz me about it.

"Why won't you see me on Sunday evening."

"I told you," I said, "I do something else on Sunday evenings."

He said, "My mates think you're seeing someone else on Sunday."

Laughing, I said, "Well, I'm not, so just leave it."

One evening we came home from a night out. There was a note addressed to me on the floor that a member of the group had dropped through my door to say that the meditation evening on Sunday was cancelled. My boyfriend knew then what I did on Sunday, but he couldn't understand why I refused to tell him. I couldn't explain it, either. Perhaps it was just too precious to bandy about. I didn't want it to be the source of an argument or be asked to give it up.

My love of things spiritual and Buddhism, in particular, caused problems with boyfriends. One man really disliked this aspect of me and wanted me to give it up. He would tell me regularly that my obsession with Buddhism was causing me to run away from life. I never understood what he meant. Chris was intelligent and I enjoyed being with him. A big part of me wanted this relationship to work. He told me on a regular basis that he didn't understand me, or the way I thought. His words began to play on my mind and I worried that there was something weird about me. For the first time in my life, I entertained the possibility of taking a drug to try to understand how my mind operated. I reasoned to myself, *If I were to smoke some marijuana, maybe I'd see what was in my mind and I'd understand what to do or how to change, so my relationship with Chris could work.*

I had a friend who smoked marijuana on a regular basis. I called him, explained the problems I was having with Chris in our relationship, and asked him to bring some pot over for me. Wayne was amazed because although he often smoked when he came to visit, I never joined him. He agreed to come over the following Saturday. All day, I waited on tenterhooks for him to arrive. I knew that I was taking a huge step. Up to that point, I had never taken anything stronger than a pain tablet for a headache. He arrived at 7:00 PM, said that he couldn't get any marijuana, but had a substitute. He reached into the breast pocket of his jacket and pulled out a small plastic bag containing what looked to me like tiny gravy granules.

"What are they?" I asked.

"They are similar to marijuana," he replied.

I accepted what he said. He opened the packet and handed me one and popped one in his own mouth. I swallowed mine and we sat on the sofa in my sitting room, waiting, although I didn't really know what we were waiting for.

"Do you see those triangles that are on your curtains?" asked Wayne after a while. I looked at him, baffled.

"What triangles?" I asked. He was quiet, obviously seeing things I couldn't.

"Look at the shapes on the floor," he said.

By this stage, I had determined that what we had taken was some kind of hallucinogenic. From my years studying psychology, I knew about the different kinds of drugs, so I didn't panic. When I told Wayne that I wasn't seeing what he was seeing, he went into a kind of panic and asked me if he could use my phone. I agreed and followed him out to the kitchen.

I heard him say to the person on the other end, "I've given her a Class A drug and it's having no effect." It was a form of LSD called STP – Serenity, Tranquility and Peace.

I didn't stay to listen to any more. I was horrified at what I had taken and hugely grateful that it had had no effect on me. Wayne came back and wanted me to take another but I said absolutely no way, that I was not taking any more, so he popped another one into his mouth. Then, the drug suddenly started to work on me. I saw the shapes on the curtains; and, on the floor, and then something strange happened. Solid objects in my flat began to change their shapes and re-form. My door became a slab of butter. I was so intrigued because, to me, this was Buddhism showing me its theory that nothing is what we think it is, that everything is changing and impermanent. So while Wayne was freaking out at the things he was seeing, I remained calm and confident.

This is not to say I endorse taking hallucinogenic drugs on a regular basis. I do not. A hallucinogenic drug only hampers expanding consciousness. The alteration of consciousness I achieved by ingesting this drug gave me something to aim for by natural means. It gave me the direct experience of seeing that nothing is as real and permanent as we think it is. Everything depends on our perception.

Plato once said something to the effect that *ordinary people are like prisoners permanently trapped in a dark cave and forced to watch a shadow puppet play, which they think is real.*

"Don't be afraid, this is exactly what Buddhism teaches," I kept saying to Wayne, who had become fearful of what he was seeing.

But he had neither the philosophical framework I had nor any spiritual context for managing altered perceptions. Without a context for interpreting such experiences, fear is a likely response. He couldn't handle how the drug was altering his perception of the world.

He kept saying, "I hope this drug doesn't make it onto the streets."

During the experience, I saw my yucca plant dance. Since I saw it dance, I can no longer look at that plant in the same way. Every time I water it, I say, "I've seen you dance."

Wayne and I went out for a walk because it was a lovely summer's night. I was struck by how lit up everything was or seemed to be; it was all so beautiful. We returned home and talked until the early hours of the morning. Then Wayne went home. I walked him to the bus stop and was amazed at how serene everything was. Except for the humans we encountered, that is. Every human being we passed was in some way deformed. Their shoulders were hunched or their faces seemed out of proportion.

This impression startled me, and has continued to affect me, and I don't know why.

I said goodbye to Wayne at the bus stop and thanked him for making it possible for me to see the potentiality of my own mind. I didn't know if it was going to improve my relationship with Chris. I didn't care. The drug had shifted my perception. My view of the world would never be the same again. I returned home and caught up on some much-needed sleep. When I woke, I noticed that I was calm and had a feeling of power. I had new confidence and felt that I could do anything.

My brother and his wife came to visit me the next evening, and I must have been spaced out because Cathy immediately asked me what I had been doing. I told her about Wayne and the drug. She was furious with me, delivered a long lecture, telling me I was lucky that the drug had been uncontaminated, and how stupid I'd been for taking something I knew nothing about. I was amazed at how strong her concern was. I promised her that it wouldn't happen again and it never did. I knew enough about Buddhism to know what had happened to me was meant to show me what is possible without drugs.

I also know that this part of my experience is controversial, and I have thought long and hard about whether or not to include it. Not to reveal it would be to deny an important part of my spiritual journey, so I decided include it. There are schools of thought that believe that the altered consciousness arising from drugs is *pseudo* and does not last. I agree with this to a point. Taking a drug shifts perception so that reality is seen in a different way. This is not the state of enlightenment; it is only a glimpse. Once this shift happens, it remains in memory. There is a big difference between permanent enlightenment and catching only a glimpse. If it were possible to become enlightened in a normal state of consciousness, it would probably be much more common.

Because the effect of the drug encourages the desire to have the experience over and over again, the first expansion of consciousness arising from either a drug or a spontaneous mystical/spiritual experience is a dangerous point in the spiritual journey. If this craving is acted on, the remainder of the spiritual journey is, at best, delayed or at worst, lost. Taking a drug within the philosophical context of expanding consciousness is a first step. The next step is pursuing it naturally through study and meditation. Some people will disagree with this stance, but my own experience at least validates it for me. Taking the drug gave me a deeper understanding of Buddhism. What I hadn't bargained for was the drug helping me to understand more *about* Buddhism. I had taken it solely to improve my relationship with Chris. Looking back, I now realize it was some kind of spiritual lesson or initiation.

Over the next week,, I continued to feel the effects of the STP, experiencing a flow to life, an ease and calmness that hadn't been there before. Everything was going right. I felt happy, relaxed, and free. Gradually, its effects wore off and life returned to its usual hectic state. Once again, I was insecure, not knowing what was going on, my mind running around like a confused child. How different it all seemed under STP!

Once or twice I thought about calling Wayne to see if he had any more, but I recognized that I was being tested as to whether I could control this desire. If I gave into temptation and took it again, it would be a disaster for my spiritual journey, so I told myself *no*. To take it a second time would be succumbing to a desire to repeat the mystical/spiritual experience, and that would go against every Buddhist principle I had — something I refused to do. When I took the drug, my intentions were clear. Asking for marijuana and being given a hallucinogenic was the result of a certain naivety, a kind of karmic joke I'd played on myself.

After this, my relationship with Chris seemed unimportant and it ended shortly after taking STP. I wasn't prepared to give up my spiritual quest. I was now on a mission to achieve an altered state of consciousness without using drugs. Buddhism became even more special to me; it came before everything and everyone else. I remember the first time I went home to my parents with some Buddhist books and explained the philosophy to them. My mother was not happy, but when she saw that I continued to go to Mass with them when I went home to visit, and I hadn't lost my job or dropped out of society, she accepted it.

GOING DEEPER

"Reason comes from an intention to know the truth."
~ Author

As time went on, I became more involved with the Buddhist organization, which meant more contact with its founder. Every couple of months we went to his home for an intense meditation retreat after which he would join us for meals. It didn't matter how often I saw him, I never felt comfortable. There was something not right about how subservient other people acted around him. I saw the normally feisty independent Sempais turn into small children around him. All I could see was how they were giving their power away. I didn't ask questions or challenge him because he was sharp and ruthless I knew he would humiliate me if I tried. I watched him do it to others.

It got to the point where the conflict between what I was learning about the wisdom and compassion of Buddhism, and the behavior of the founder became too much. I started to voice my concerns to others in the group about him and his methods of teaching. This changed the whole energy within the group. Suddenly, I was a troublemaker. I wasn't high up in the pecking order because I had only been a member for a couple of years. Others in the group began to resent me voicing my concerns. I was regularly told that my ego was the problem. This caused me much worry.

In the end, I left, unable to reconcile the differences between the head of the organization's lack of compassion and the central role compassion plays in Buddhist theory. But I was to return three times before I finally left. At that stage, I had been studying with the group for nine years. Quitting had a huge impact. For a long time after, my life felt empty without the Monday and Thursday evening Kempo classes, the yoga class on Saturday, and the meditation class on Sunday. During this time, I was racked by self-doubt. Had I done the right thing? Why couldn't my ego be as subservient as the others? Why didn't they see what I saw in this man — the contradictions and inconsistencies between what Buddhism says and practices, and what he said and practiced? How could I be the only one to see it?

What I didn't know was the effect that my voicing concerns would eventually have on Andrew, the person who first introduced me to the group. He slowly began to see the leader in a different light and to challenge him in a way he had never dared to do before. This was particularly difficult for him because Andrew had been his student for 18 years. The reaction of the leader was to expel Andrew from the group. A few years later, the organization folded — its founder dead after being convicted of sexual abuse — all of which left its followers bewildered and bitter about the years they'd spent devoted to a guru who turned out to have feet of clay.

Googling the name of this organization still brings up a discussion forum of past students, trying to understand what went wrong. I rejected the idea of finding another teacher. I resolved to become my own teacher. I was determined to go it alone. In my mind, all teachers were corrupt. I had seen well-meaning and well-intentioned people exploited by a cynical, self-deluded man. It angered and saddened me. It was particularly upsetting to read a posting from a student who had spent many years with the founder, saying that he has lost the motivation and enthusiasm for life that being a part of the organization had given to him.

After leaving the group, I lost contact with everybody. I felt I had been the cause of the movement breaking down, but did not know that for sure. Before I arrived, the group had been operating comfortably for many years. I came along and started asking questions and pointing certain things out. Slowly, but surely, the whole thing tumbled like a house of cards. I felt vindicated, relieved that my gut feeling had proven right. It strengthened my commitment to go it alone without any teacher.

Soon after, I was offered the choice of redundancy at work or a change of position within the company. The position I was offered was "number cruncher." My heart sank. Given my weakness with numbers and logic, accepting the job was inviting failure.

So I accepted redundancy. My study of Buddhism had nurtured a desire to visit India. And I saw redundancy as a karmic invitation to do so. I wanted to do a retreat in India. I found a meditation center, which ran retreats in southern England as well as in India.

A VISIT TO INDIA

"Breaking away from a structure is common in the lives of realized people."
~ Author

I wasn't supposed to follow this path. I was brought up as a good Catholic girl. Mass every Sunday and regular reminders of how I would be punished by God if I didn't behave. However, after I discovered Buddhism in 1988, I studied its ideas and practices for the next nine years. In 1996, I decided that it was time to throw away the books and commit myself to some serious practice. India seemed like a good choice as it was where the Buddha became enlightened. Who knows? Some of its magic might rub off on me!

I contacted the center and said I wanted to do a meditation retreat in India. They told me about one in the Thai monastery in Bodhgaya. I wanted to see the place because the Buddha became enlightened here, and I wanted to visit some of the important places he had sojourned. For everything it had given me, I dedicated my trip to the Buddha and Buddhism.

The registration forms were sent to me and I signed up for a 10-day silent Vipassana (insight) meditation retreat in Bodhgaya in January 1997. I was both excited and apprehensive because I had never done a long, silent meditation retreat or been backpacking alone before. I had completed weekend retreats with the Buddhist organization, but they weren't silent. This retreat was to be completely silent. There would be no study like the Sunday evenings I loved, but my resolve was strong. Since my inner voice had warned me about the London organization and urged me to leave it, I was filled with gratitude and I wanted to do something significant in return.

So, on January 6, 1997, I set off for India. My first stop was Delhi. I arrived at 2:00 AM. I was lucky to have friends, who, when they heard I didn't have any accommodations booked, insisted on booking a hotel that offered airport pickup for transport to and from the hotel. When I disembarked the plane at Delhi airport, I was thankful to see my name scrawled on a piece of cardboard.

I woke up the next morning feeling refreshed and ready to explore the city. I left the hotel, feeling immediate panic on the street due my poor sense of direction. There was no point in my taking a map because I can't read one — another left brain thing — reading maps. Taking a deep breath, I headed away from the hotel. Walking down shanty streets, I lost count of the people begging. Mothers holding small, emaciated children with forlorn brown eyes. I knew I couldn't give to one and not another. To do this would invite an army of beggars, making it impossible for me to walk around Delhi.

I stayed in Delhi for a couple of days and then travelled to Bodhgaya for the retreat. Arriving early at the Thai monastery, I walked through the gates and saw people walking slowly, looking down at the ground. I remember thinking: *Why are all these people walking with their heads down when it's such a lovely day?* One of the tutors saw me and came over. I explained that I was here for the retreat. He said that registration didn't begin until 3:00 PM. He asked me politely if could I go away and come back closer to the time, because the previous retreat was not yet over. I agreed, once again shouldering my rucksack. As I sat in a street stall, taking in the sights of Bodhgaya, I marveled at the number of Buddhist and Tibetan monks in this small city, a number only exceeded by the amount of religious merchandise on display.

Shortly before 3:00 PM, I returned to find a queue of people, all western, waiting to register. There wasn't even one Indian among the waiting. After completing the formalities, I was shown to a dormitory with six straw mats on a concrete floor, a traditional Indian toilet, and a sink. I put my sleeping bag on a straw mat in the corner. I had marked my territory. There was another sleeping bag in the other corner, so I knew I wasn't going to be alone. I walked out to explore my surroundings. Turning the corner, I saw a notice board. One of the posts said the first meeting would be in the hall at 7:00 that evening. I went looking for the hall. Inside, I saw an assortment of cushions, shawls, meditation stools, and blankets, all arranged in different positions by people who had registered earlier and reserved their place. I realized I'd better do the same so I went to the back of the hall where the cushions, blankets, and stools were stacked.

Since I prefer to meditate on a stool, I took one, along with a couple of cushions and a blanket and then went to mark my place.

At 7:00 PM we assembled in the hall, ready to meet the teachers, who would be with us for the next 10 days, and listen to the introductory talk about practicalities, giving up passports and money, and so on. There were no mobile phones in those days. The timetable for each day was on the notice board. There was to be no writing or keeping of journals. Silence was to be kept at all times. Each day, there would be two verbal sessions: a question and answer session at 2:00 PM and a dharma (Buddha wisdom) talk at 7:00 PM. On alternate days, there were small group meetings where participants could discuss any aspect of the retreat. The teachers were available for one-on-one talks at specific times, should anyone need to speak to them. I reckoned there were about 350 people doing the retreat and again, was amazed that not one of them was Indian-born.

Each day began at 5:00 AM with an hour and a half yoga session. The number of yoga postures I can do is limited. Postures like the *camel* and *headstands* are pure agony, but I resolved to go every morning. I had promised myself to give this retreat everything I had. After yoga, we had breakfast, which was usually porridge with honey. After breakfast, there was a clean-up session for an hour where we all had tasks. I can't remember what mine was — possibly because there were so many of us, I got away without doing anything. After the tasks, there was a sitting meditation that lasted for 45 minutes and then a walking meditation outside. I was amazed at the difference between the two meditations. I found the sitting meditation very difficult. Every minute was like an hour. It brought back memories of my meditations in north London as part of the Buddhist organization. I sat and looked at everyone around me, deep in something I was not a part of. I wondered, for the umpteenth time, what I was missing.

But the walking meditations were a different story. Ambling outside in the warm sunshine with roses and water lilies scattered around the paths, I found it easy to be aware and present. I felt connected with the sky and the trees. I couldn't explain why but my feelings of joy and contentment were real. I could walk outside forever. The meditation was particularly powerful for me because my feet were connected to the earth. Lifting one foot slowly and with gentle awareness, placing it on the earth, and then doing the same with the other foot, the moment of that connection with the earth was very powerful and never failed to move me. After the walking meditation, the bell rang to signify another sitting and, oh, how different it would be! My mind would start to deny what was happening and bring up all sorts of questions: "What am I doing here?" "It's all a load of rubbish." My mind and I would battle back and forth.

It was agony; I vowed to skip the next sitting. Then the bell rang, signaling outdoor walking meditation and all my angst disappeared in the warm sunshine. I forgot the agony of sitting until once again, I was sitting. We had two main meals: breakfast and lunch. Dinner was tea and fruit around 4:30 PM. After lunch, we had another sitting meditation and then a question and answer session. I willed people to ask questions. If they didn't, we'd have another sitting meditation. I used to breathe a sigh of relief when the leader asked: "Any questions?"

Someone would always pipe up. I loved these question and answer sessions. Because of the years I had spent dabbling with the occult using tarot cards, I was curious about whether or not there is a difference between psychic and spiritual. Intuitively I felt there was, but was unable to explain why.

At one of the sessions, I asked the leader. "I don't think they're two separate things; they're more like two sides of the same coin," he said.

This made me think, but before I had time to reply, he thanked me and began the customary silence before requesting the next question.

After the question and answer session, there was a second walking meditation and then a break for tea after which, more meditation. At 7:00 PM, one of the teachers gave a talk on some aspect of the Buddha's teaching, which was followed by a final walking meditation. I particularly loved this part of the retreat because it was dark outside. The sky was clear with the moon in full view. I looked up and thought about something the teacher had said during his talk. It was all so perfect – for the first five days, at least!

MIND BEGINS TO BITE

"When we surrender with good grace, without any resentment and with love, conditions arise that enable a shift to occur."

~ Author

For the first five days, I was busy watching people; everyone looks interesting when they don't speak. Mentally, I tagged the people I would speak with when the silence was broken. On day six, I was getting anxious and agitated. The sitting meditations hadn't gotten any better and the walking ones were becoming boring, in spite of the beauty of the Thai monastery and its surroundings.

Questions like *Why are you wasting time with this?* kept gnawing at me. I tried to quell them, but the more I resisted the stronger they got. By day eight I thought I was going mad. The silence was driving me insane and I couldn't stop the voice in my head from mocking this retreat.

I knew that after breakfast some of the participants brought food from the kitchen to feed young Indian children who would gather at the gates of the monastery. One morning I went down to see what went on. Walking down I saw a line of young children that extended way back towards Bodhgaya — kids from the village queuing outside the monastery gates.

The gates were opened and a stream of children came running onto the grounds and formed a line. The children were given biscuits that morning. I lined up with one little girl who didn't speak any English. She put her hand in mine and kept smiling up at me. We walked towards the front of the queue and as we approached, I saw one volunteer look worried. The little girl and I were second from the top when the person giving out the biscuits said: "No more biscuits."

I couldn't believe it. I looked down at this little girl who had her hand so trustingly in mine and didn't know what to say. I was on retreat and I couldn't leave it to buy biscuits for her. I just released my hand from hers. I will never forget the look of sadness mixed with resignation that she gave me. I thought that my heart would break, but what came over me was pure anger. I turned to go back to the monastery and saw one of the leaders of the retreat walking alongside me. Unable to control myself, I blurted out: "What we are doing here is so self-indulgent when outside these gates there are starving children."

He continued walking as though he hadn't heard me. What else could I expect on a silent retreat? He wasn't going to break the rules to reassure or comfort me. I walked back into the meditation hall, spent the time crying and thinking how wrong everything was outside the monastery gates. Putting aside my anger was difficult. I felt so selfish. My mind was in such turmoil I put a note on the board asking to speak to one of the teachers. I was in crisis, my mind and emotions were all over the place. I had lost all objectivity.

I met with one of the leaders, a woman. When I told her how I felt, she didn't seem to see the fact that a little child went hungry as the unacceptable event I saw it to be. She talked only about the depth of compassion and empathy I felt towards the situation. The way I allowed myself to be moved and touched by the event. I felt that her answer was cold and unfeeling. I didn't see how she could view the compassion I felt as more important than the child missing out on biscuits. I couldn't see her viewpoint at all; it only added to the agitation I was already feeling.

At the end of the eighth day, I'd had enough. I was going to leave. I reasoned that I'd be travelling around India for another three months and it was more important to take care of my mental state. I didn't feel in control of my emotions and was scared about the toll it was taking on my mind.

Then, without thinking about it, I stopped fighting with my mind. Accepting my fear, facing it, I experienced a peace and calm I had never felt before. It was surprising and totally unexpected. I went to bed wondering how I would feel in the morning. When I woke up, the peace and calm were still there. All mental agitation was gone. Delighted, I got up, renewed and refreshed, in time for yoga. Over the next few days, the incident of the child at the gate still bothered me so one day after breakfast a thought prompted me to go down again to the gate, but I resisted. I didn't want to go through it again; but, the thought persisted, so I went down. That morning eggs were being given out to the children, but they didn't seem as hungry today as a couple of mornings earlier. They were throwing the eggs like balls. I saw the situation differently and was glad I had taken the risk and gone back into what I had decided was an upsetting situation.

The rest of the retreat was easier. The sitting meditations were better because the agitation in my mind had vanished. I was grateful. I knew I would stay for the rest of the retreat.

Fighting with the mind prevents a state of peace and calm from emerging; accepting fear, not fighting against it in any way enables something else to emerge. Putting an end to the struggle with my mind by accepting my emotions created a shift that allowed me to experience another state of consciousness. Only after surrendering with good grace, without any resentment and with love, were conditions for an insightful shift able to develop.

There was the opportunity to stay on and do another 10 days of the retreat.

"Why don't you stay?" my inner voice asked. "Now that you have this nice peaceful and calm state, there's no telling what you might achieve." For a short time, I was tempted. But then I remembered the promise I had made to myself and said, "No, I committed myself to a ten-day retreat and that's what I'm going to do."

Our nature wants pleasurable moments to continue, and moments that are not as pleasurable to stop. Because I wanted the pleasure to continue, I was in danger of falling into this trap when tempted by a second 10 days. The spiritual path is all about recognising these tendencies, not judging them or saying that they are wrong — just noticing them.

The final day I awoke for yoga with joy in my heart. I had done it. I had completed a 10-day silent meditation retreat and survived. This was no mean feat for me because I love to talk. Before the retreat, not speaking for long periods of time was inconceivable.

The silence was to be broken at midday after a talk about being gentle with ourselves when we go back out into the world. This meant not bursting into too much talk, too soon. First allowing ourselves time to become accustomed to life outside the monastery. Once we could talk, to my absolute amazement I found I wanted to talk, but couldn't. I knew what I wanted to say, but the words wouldn't come.

I also found the din of everyone talking overwhelming. I took myself to a quiet part of the monastery to try to understand what had happened. Where was my desire to talk to all of these people, to share experiences and be part of the community? The noise was just too much. I was suddenly reminded of the old adage *speech is silver, but silence is golden*. Not only golden but incredibly powerful, underestimated in its ability to enable shifts in consciousness. Since then, keeping some silent time in my life has been important. This retreat taught me the most profound transformation happens through silence, not speech.

Silence has a powerful, spiritually transformational effect. In silence, the mind has nowhere to go and eventually gives up to reveal a hidden state of peace and calm. But it doesn't do this easily. For me, a silent retreat was essential in breaking the hold the mind has over consciousness. Before I did the intensive 10-day silent retreat, I had been on the occasional weekend meditation retreat and had meditated a little every day, but it was subjecting my mind to continual silence, to the point where I became so agitated and distressed, almost to the point of exhaustion, that I finally gave up, inducing a complete shift of consciousness.

Looking back at that retreat: What I went through was a street fight with myself (my mind) and this is what I believe it takes to become spiritually awakened, to get into a street fight with yourself. But who wants to do that?

LIFE AFTER THE RETREAT

"We are spiritual beings come to earth to have human experiences."

~ Author

After the retreat, I was amazed and full of gratitude for the shift that occurred, thankful that I hadn't gotten ill during the 10 days — quite rare for a western traveler in India! I packed my rucksack and headed to Bodhgaya for a couple of days before setting off for Calcutta. One day, I was sitting outside a *chai* (Indian tea) shop reading a book on compassion when I became aware of a tapping on my toe. Looking down, I saw a naked, crippled boy, gazing up at me and holding his hand out, begging. I stared down at him, shook my head, and continued reading my book. I didn't give it another thought. It was only the next day when I was without the book on compassion that I saw the same boy surrounded by monks who were dressing and feeding him. With shame, I saw the chance I had missed to demonstrate compassion instead of just reading about it. That lesson has stayed with me. There is a danger in investing so much in books that when the real thing comes along, ready to be experienced, we are blind to it. We allow books to replace experience. They are good pointers, but no substitute for experience.

After leaving Bodhgaya, I arrived in Calcutta. I wanted to work for Mother Teresa's organization, so I registered with them and was assigned to an orphanage in the slums of Howrah just outside Calcutta. Every morning, I took the bus, then walked a mile through the slums to the orphanage with a couple of other people. I had never journeyed through such areas of poverty and felt a lump in my throat each morning, wondering what causes such poverty here when there is so much affluence in the world. The orphanage was heartbreaking, full of little children that had just been left there. Since they had no toys or anything to play with, I went to a toyshop in Calcutta and bought plastic rings and other things and gave them to the sisters, but in all the time I was there, I never saw those toys being given to the children. I used to ask, but they just smiled at me and say, "Yes, sister." In the end, I gave up asking.

After Calcutta, I travelled to Varanasi, formerly Benares. I was standing on one of the many *ghats*, the steps going down to the Ganges, the most sacred river in India, when a man asked me if I would like to see his guru. Being open minded, I said yes, so he brought me to a small hut. I walked inside and saw an old man who looked at me intently. He told me a reading was $25.00, which I handed over. Then he said I had lost a child. I knew this wasn't true, but thought I would check with him and said, "In this life?"

He said, "Yes, in this life."

I knew then this man was a fraud and I was angry with myself for having been taken in. I left soon afterwards, but it tarnished my image of Varanasi.

The next day I was at another of the *ghats*, the Burning Ghat, where the bodies of the dead are burned. Funerals in India are a joyous affair, not like in the West. The body is brought down on a stretcher, dressed in bright colors, and the relatives sing and dance. They place the body on a wood pyre and then burn it. It takes eight hours for a body to burn. No cameras are allowed at this Ghat. I was standing in a tower high above the Ghat watching a burning body when I heard a man beside me scream and run from the tower. When I looked down, he had grabbed a camera from a tourist who had been trying to take a picture, ignoring the sign that read "NO CAMERAS." Eventually, the angry man returned it to the tourist who had blatantly disregarded the sign.

I didn't blame him, revealing my own feelings. "Tourists like that give Westerners a bad name," I said.

He gave me a strange look, then said, "Would you like to come and visit my guru?" I exploded with anger and said, "What is it with you people; why do you prey on tourists like this?"

He looked shocked and so I told him about the other man who had charged $25.00 and told me lies. When I finished, he said, "You come; no money."

"What, no money?" I repeated, and he said, "Yes."

I agreed to go with him. I don't know why. Now I realize I was searching for answers outside of me, only to be thrown back on myself each time. I had the answers within me, but refused to acknowledge them at that time. I would accept and investigate, but if something didn't make sense, I would expose weakness (like I had with the London Buddhist leader). Not having a teacher, I adopted the universe as my teacher and constructed a philosophy around the signs from this Great Source. Going with this stranger was yet another unfiltered sign.

When we arrived at the home of a younger man, his presence gripped me the moment I laid eyes on him. I felt awe and respect for this person I had never met. He had the brownest of eyes that seemed to look right into my soul. He had a power I could not deny. I don't remember much of what he told me, only that he looked intently into my eyes and said that life would get better. He said that he had something he wanted to give me. With the memory of how I had been deceived still fresh in my mind, I thought to myself, *Oh no, not again.*

"How much?" I asked.

"Ten rupees (20p) a donation," he replied, "I will say you are a pupil of mine, but you have to come and get it tomorrow afternoon at 2:00."

I agreed to go back the next day to collect whatever it was he wanted to give me. My lodgings were far away from this man's dwelling. *It's only 10 rupees*, I thought, *I won't go and get it.* But a powerful, stronger inner voice said: *Go and get it, it's important.* At 2:00 PM, I was sitting beside this man whose power seemed so palpable. On impulse, I had stopped and bought some Indian sweets that I gave him. He would only take one, as would his assistant, the man who had brought me to him the previous day. He handed me what looked like a small barrel covered with red material and told me to wear it, I thanked him and gave him the 10 rupees. Suddenly, I had an overpowering urge to take his photograph. It seemed important for me to do this. I asked him if I could and he agreed. I took the picture and went away. I didn't think any more about it. I saw him a couple of times while walking around Varanasi and every time, I was struck by something in his presence. He had an ease and grace about him. Each time, we met he acknowledged me with a smile, but nothing more.

A couple of days later, I took a rickshaw to Sarnath, a park outside Varanasi where the Buddha gave his first lecture after becoming enlightened. I was struck by how quiet and calm places associated with the Buddha are, compared to how busy everywhere else in India is. This place was no exception. I took a couple of photographs and then left.

My next step: Delhi to Nepal and then onto Lumbini where the Buddha was born. Lumbini was very quiet. A little boy attached himself to me as I walked around. When I stopped to eat an orange, I gave him half. He sat down quite contented, which instilled a deep sense of joy and inner peace in me. Was it a remnant of the peace and calm that emerged during the retreat? I don't know, but since I'd left Bodhgaya, everything seemed to flow. Everything worked. I didn't miss trains. Someone always helped me when I was unsure about what to do.

In India, the people are lovely, with one exception: To secure a place on a train, they'll knock you over. Anything that gets in their way is pushed aside in the mad rush to board. Once, while waiting for a train from Lumbini to Pokara, I was worried because I didn't know how far up the train my carriage to Pokara was. I was on the station platform when a man came up to me. He was reading a book and asked me about some words. I started to read with him, showing him how to read the words by breaking them into syllables. The man watched me glance at my ticket from time to time and must have sensed my anxiety because, as soon as the train came, he took my ticket, got on the train, and motioned me through the window to follow him along the platform, which I did. He walked through the carriages until he stopped at a seat and then beckoned me to get on the train. I was so overwhelmed by his kindness I didn't know what to say. I offered him some rupees, but he refused. I was very grateful. We shook hands, smiled at one another, then said goodbye. Incidents like this, which are quite common, make India a special place for me.

From my time in India, I learned that I have all the answers within. Ultimately, the learning place, the laboratory, is inside my own being. It's not in a hut in India or an ashram in the heart of London — it's within me. I also learned that accepting fear could transform the struggle in my mind. After four incredible months, I returned to London.

BACK IN LONDON

"One day, I intuitively knew that I was no longer walking the path; I was the path."

~ Author

I can't help comparing London to India, where I'd travelled on the back of rickshaws at all hours of the day and night, with all my possessions, without ever feeling any threat to my safety.

When I landed at Heathrow Airport, it was night. I took a taxi back to my flat. The driver went down back streets I wasn't familiar with. For the first time in four months, I felt fear. The darkness I'd been so at ease with in India was now something to be afraid of. I put my key to the keyhole only to find it didn't fit. Confused, I called a friend who explained that my flat had been burgled and my brother had changed the locks. She suggested I stay with her while I got in touch with him. When I eventually got into my flat, I found all my gold jewelry, of which I had plenty, had been stolen. From that moment on, I lost all interest in expensive jewelry.

I began looking for a job, building up a network of friends; in short, I started over from the beginning. I took a series of fleeting jobs while figuring out what to do with my life. Eventually, I got a short-term contract in a motor vehicle company. From the moment I walked into their motorcycle division, I knew I wanted to be there. A buzz about the department excited me, and the people who worked there were friendly.

Working in the private sector was a huge shock after being in the public sector for so many years. For the first couple of months, I was exhausted at the end of every day. Spiritually, I was at a crossroads. I didn't know what to do. I felt that I had gone as far as I could with Buddhism. I was also frustrated at why I couldn't put into words what I understood intuitively. My understanding of spiritual literature was so complete in my own mind, but when I tried to communicate with others, it never came out the way I wanted.

I wondered why I believed I needed to be able to communicate. Did I feel a need to proselytize? I knew I didn't want knowledge and understanding only for myself alone. I wanted to be able to touch and inspire people, and this wasn't happening. One morning, I was standing in my bedroom, looking out of my window, thinking about my situation, when my inner voice said *give it up*. That's it, three words, no suggestion of what else to do, just those three little authoritative words.

My heart sank when I thought about how much of my life I had invested, almost twenty-five years, in self-realization. Nevertheless, I listened to that prompt which was more like an order and gave up any plans to read spiritual books, attend conferences or workshops, or enter into any spiritual discussions. Words can't describe the hollowness I felt. Since the age of 11 I had thought about, read about, and tried to understand this path that mystics throughout the ages had spoken about. Now I reasoned that I was being asked to "give it up" because I had come as far as my karma would allow for this lifetime. I could accept this inner instruction because of my strong belief in karma and reincarnation.

Every act we perform produces karma which, put simply, is the result of our actions and our thoughts. Reincarnation is an ongoing process, the result of the karma we have accumulated over many lifetimes. I looked at this prompt as a coming to the end of what I could learn during this lifetime. To go further, I had to ensure that from this point on my thoughts and actions would produce beneficial karma so that the next time I was reborn, I could continue where I had left off. The fact that I didn't have a conscious understanding of spiritual truths also convinced me that I had come as far as I could in this lifetime. I believed that conscious understandings of spiritual truths were for saints and mystics — or even fast-talking charlatans — but not for ordinary people like me. I also reasoned that if I couldn't have the kind of understanding by which people could learn from me, I should give it up.

Ending all spiritual seeking coincided with meeting a guy who was to shake my world in a way no man ever had up to then. He was younger than I and we became friends. He had a girlfriend who he talked to me about. One day, he came into work and announced that it was over between Rachel, his girlfriend, and him. I was sympathetic and said something philosophical like, "If it is meant to be, it will be." I didn't feel anything about this news. We always went to lunch together and this day I called him as usual for lunch. To my surprise, he said that Mary from personnel was coming with us as well. As he said this, I felt my stomach give a sickening thud. I didn't understand what it was, but I could only pick at my lunch and soon made my apologies and left them. Walking outside, I talked to myself to try to understand the origin of my strong feelings. Simple really: I was jealous.

Back in the office that afternoon, I was now wary of the person who had been a good friend, and knew that my feelings for him had moved on from friendship without my being aware of it. During the afternoon, he came to my desk and asked me if I was okay, that I'd been "a bit funny at lunch." I couldn't say anything, only look at him. Shaking his head, he returned to his desk.

Now I was scared. Something was happening that I couldn't control. Up to then, I'd had boyfriends, but had never had a reaction like the one this guy triggered in me. I was scared of him and began to find ways not to be with him. But he didn't seem to notice anything was different and kept up the cozy friendship we had, telling me about different girls he had been out with, now that he was single. Each one he mentioned was like a knife going through my heart. Once, I'd lived for seeing him in the morning; now, the early hours were times of agony. What scared me most was the quiet way my feelings for him had built up without my being the least bit aware. It was ironic, given my years of Buddhism, which is all about developing self-awareness. I found it more difficult to hide my feelings, but he kept up the easy friendship, which only increased my confusion. The turmoil became so great that I thought perhaps, if we got together, I could get this guy out of my system. For the first time, I was in a situation that I was unable to control.

One weekend, we were asked to work a show outside London. On Sunday, he asked me if I wanted a lift back to London. I agreed happily. Driving back, it was the clearest, starriest of nights. The music of Bruce Springsteen blared from the car speakers. In that moment, I realized I had never been so happy and was gripped with a mad urgency to tell him how I felt. He must have sensed something because he suddenly asked, "Are you happy on your own?"

I thought before replying. "Up to now I was."

I didn't elaborate because I couldn't. I didn't have the words. He didn't probe further and we continued driving in peaceful, companionable silence. As we got closer to London, I hoped that my flatmate would be out so we could have the place to ourselves. But when we came around the corner, I saw the light on in the sitting room, and realized that we wouldn't be alone. He pulled up outside the house and I invited him in for coffee. We sat in the kitchen, in separate chairs, and I told him how I felt about him. It was a surreal situation and he didn't know what to say. He said he'd had no idea, that he would "think about it," and then he stood up to leave. Now that I had pressed the self-destruct button, there was no turning back. I opened the door to my bedroom, sat him down on the bed, and kissed him. I felt him go rigid with shock. At that point, something penetrated through to my consciousness and I came to my senses. *This is no good, just let him go*, I thought.

"See you at work tomorrow," he said as he left.

I was horrified at what I had done because it was so unlike me. I went into the sitting room to my flatmate and told her what had happened, but all she did was laugh. Needless to say, I got precious little sleep that night. I dreaded going into work the next day. What had come over me? Where had these feelings come from? Although I was 35, I'd never had them before. More importantly, why couldn't I control them? The next day when I arrived at work, I found him there before me. He greeted me with a big smile.

"Just in time for breakfast!" he announced cheerfully. I smiled wanly. "About last night..." he said, over breakfast.

"Yes?"

He told me that it was good, but that there were "rules" because we worked together so we'd have to be discreet. I happily agreed. I was relieved and wondered what the next step would be, when we'd get together. At work, I was on tenterhooks all the time, something new for me. Eventually, after much arranging, we did get together. While I was the happiest I had ever been with a guy, something was missing. I couldn't extend the deep feelings I had for him to have satisfying sex; I was tense and nervous and had no idea why. Here I was an adult and yet, I felt like an awkward child. It was like I had invested so much in my spiritual development for so long that my emotional development was stunted.

This was frustrating for me and for him. We saw each other less and less. I had resigned myself to thinking that it was over when our manager asked us if we would work on a Saturday morning to clear a backlog. I was amazed at this turn of events and thought *this is meant to be; why else would it have happened?* and I became excited. Both of us agreed to work, and I started to plan. I had mapped out what we'd do together after we'd finished work and how everything would be great. I was beside myself with anticipation. Saturday morning came and he arrived — his usual, gorgeous self.

"Hello," he said.

We worked for a while and then I heard him pick up the phone and make arrangements to see his friends that evening. When he put the phone down, he said, "Well that's my Saturday night sorted; what are you doing?"

A wave of disappointment came over me. "I thought we would be together this evening," I said.

"I don't want what you want," he said. As he spoke those words, I felt an energy rise up from within me, and I began to shake. Not an abnormal condition or convulsion, but a physical energy rocking my whole body.

"You're shaking. Are you okay?" he asked.

I desperately wanted to reassure him that I was, but I couldn't speak. I was too engrossed in what was happening within my body. All I could do — my total awareness — was focused on staying connected to the shaking.

"You're shaking. Are you okay?" he asked again, but I still couldn't answer.

After a while, the tremors ended and I could speak. I tried to start a normal conversation to put him at ease, but I was too disorientated. Whatever had happened to me had unsettled him. A few minutes later he said, "I'm going."

With a curt goodbye, he turned off his computer and left.

MAKING SENSE OF WHAT HAPPENED

"If you have no courage, don't approach the Path."
~ Author

I sat in a daze wondering what had happened. What on earth had gone on within me? What was this energy deep within, which wasn't rage or anger, just a shaking energy? I asked lots of questions of myself, but no answers came. Eventually, I turned the computer off and went home. I walked home disorientated, so into my own world I didn't see my friend arrive.

"Are you alright?" she asked, pulling at my arm.

Hesitantly, I described the burst of energy that had come up from within me. Because she knew about the situation at work and how stressed I had been because of this guy, her advice for me was to leave my job. I tried to explain that what had happened had nothing to do with this guy or my job. It was about what had happened in the depths of my body. But she wouldn't listen. I spent the rest of the weekend replaying the experience over and over in my mind, trying to identify a trigger factor for why I suddenly shook so violently, but couldn't find one.

How strange that after this release of energy, which I now understand was Kundalini, I found myself calm and relaxed. I communicated easily and everything flowed harmoniously. I couldn't understand what had happened, so to make sense of it, I went to counseling. The counselor said it sounded like I had matured emotionally – I was 35! She said that perhaps the sheltered childhood I had lived meant that I had repressed a lot of my feelings and this guy just broke through the wall I had built around myself. She said that it was shock that had caused my body to shake. At the time, I accepted her explanation and asked her how the shock had induced such a state of peace and calm in the aftermath. Why was life now so easy and effortless compared to how it was before? She had no answers, except to admit "it was strange."

Sitting in the room, trying to sort the experience out with her, I had the strongest feeling I wouldn't find what I was looking for there. That's why, when she suggested doing another six weeks, I declined. I knew deep down that the answer lay somewhere else. I can now differentiate between the ways trained medical people as opposed to spiritual adepts interpret these experiences. Trained medical people deal with the physical body. If it can't be traced to the physical body, it doesn't exist. Kundalini and the chakras are located in a metaphysical realm, the subtle energy body that with the knowledge and equipment we have today, can't be seen. Their presence has been verified by mystics, but not by science. How frustrating to experience these energy flows from the chakras, yet be unable to authenticate my experience for others!

After this, life flowed and I experienced a harmony and balance that I had never known. Prior to that Saturday morning, my mind had always been busy, agitated, continually planning, unable to stop for a minute. Suddenly, it was quiet. Previously, my communications with others were problematic; I didn't understand them and they didn't understand me. Now, communicating was relaxed and without tension. Gradually, I merged into this state of peace, calm, and serenity. Each day my communication skills grew deeper and less stressed. I realized that my experience had somehow shifted my emotional balance.

The happiest times are when something good comes from a traumatic event, and you don't know why. With no attempt to label it, the experience is enjoyed without reservation or hesitation. It had happened to me.

I kept a diary during that period that is full of wonder at how my life turned around after this experience. I would compare similar *before and after* situations — those before *the experience*, fraught and tense, and those afterwards that flowed harmoniously. It was nothing short of miraculous, an effect that takes a long time to assimilate. It was like my mind had shifted completely.

When I look back at this experience, what caused the calmness was a clearing of energy blocking the first three chakras or energy centers of the body. The chakras are vortices of energy along the spine in a layer called the *etheric*. Seven in number, the first three are the physical, emotional, and mental chakras. These are the lower chakras that make up our personality.

Blocked energy in any of these chakras causes tension. What Kundalini did was unblock the trapped energy in these chakras, balancing the physical, emotional, and mental aspects of my personality. My thoughts and emotions were calm and relaxed. Life flowed. My physical body became stronger. Each morning I would wake up and check to see if the state of calm was still there. When confirmed, my heart would fill with gratitude.

One evening, I was late going to meet friends and grabbed a book from my bookshelf to read. On the bus, I took the book out of my bag and my heart sank as I saw it was one of the spiritual books that I had given up reading. I renounced the spiritual path a few months after I returned from India in 1997. I thought that even being on the spiritual path was a kind of arrogance. After all, no one had specifically told me that this was a path I should be on. Even though I had always believed that the search for spiritual meaning and purpose is a universal one for all human beings, I thought I was wrong, that this path of awareness and enlightenment was only for good, spiritual people like mystics and saints, not for ordinary people like me. I had made the decision that if I was to know more, I would get some sign and thus end my search. So, to suddenly be holding a spiritual book once more filled me with a mixture of excitement and fear.

The book I had taken in such haste from my bookshelf was one I felt compelled to buy at one of the various talks or workshops I had attended at an earlier time. Excited and motivated by the talk or workshop, I had brought it home and opened up the first chapter eagerly, only to give up quickly because I couldn't understand or connect with what was written. The book went on the bookshelf with all the others, its pages barely exposed to light.

This time was different. As my eyes glided over the sentences, the words jumped out at me with new meaning and understanding. Suddenly, there was no learning involved, no struggle; the insights in the book were crystal clear and seemed to confirm a deep intuitive, unconscious knowledge within me. At that moment, everyone on the bus disappeared. I was completely absorbed by the words on the page. I was so wrapped up in the book that I forgot to get off the bus when it came to my stop. When I returned home that evening, I looked through all my books and noticed that it was the same: whichever one I opened – I had a new understanding and an ease of *reading* I hadn't had before. Surprised and delighted, I pondered what this meant. It could mean only one thing – it was the sign I had been waiting for. When I gave up all spiritual activities, I did so because my being on a spiritual journey seemed arrogant. I had never been given a direct sign I was going in the right direction. Here was the sign I had given up hope of ever getting. It was time to return to the spiritual arena.

Having been away for so long, I didn't know what to do. Should I do Buddhism again or try something else? I called Andrew, the man who had introduced me to Buddhism and told him a little about what had happened and how I wanted to do "something." He suggested a spiritual group he attended that was easy and relaxed, and recommended I go. I went for many weeks. Each time I returned home renewed. I understood everything that went on in terms of talks and meditation. Yet, although I understood everything that was said, I did not have any original insights of my own. These were to come later.

Gradually, as is common when things become too familiar, I noticed I was getting both complacent and impatient. From not reading anything for months, I now read everything I could get my hands on. Most of my understanding came from reading authors who created their books by channeled automatic writing, such as the *Conversations with God* books by Neale Donald Walsch and *A Course in Miracles* by Helen Schucman. These gave me the strongest messages and insights. At around this time, I began working as a volunteer for a mind, body, and spirit center in the heart of London.

There, with spiritual books surrounding me, it didn't matter which one I picked up. I only needed to read a paragraph to understand its meaning or find the answer to something I had been pondering. Without a teacher — because of my decision not to give my power away to anyone — books became my mentors, answering many of my questions. The biggest and longest query was whether my decision to not look for a teacher came from my ego or my soul. One evening, I picked up one of the books from the table and opened it. As usual, one line jumped out "the spiritual path is the path by the alone to the alone." I felt a great relief and took it to mean that going it alone was my path.

From my reading, it dawned on me that everything I had to say had already been said or done before in one way or another. I spent hours wondering what I could do or say that would be different, a way to shift the spiritually purposed quest into a new dimension. I put a request out to that bigger connection I've had since childhood.

What had happened on that Saturday morning in the office was spiritual. I had no doubt about it now. I knew intuitively that I was never going to find an answer through the counseling because it didn't take the spiritual dimension into account.

When I realized this, I became afraid. My mind began to voice doubts about the whole experience. *Why has it happened to me? Who am I? I'm going mad.*

I didn't have a teacher. I was reluctant to speak about what had happened so I began to think that this state of peace and calm hadn't been given to me for nothing. Something was expected from me in return. As a result, I believed that this experience and the synchronicity I enjoyed both personally and spiritually was dependent on my giving something back. I didn't know what this might be, and I was afraid. I wondered if this was a calling for me to leave so-called normal life and enter into permanent solitary confinement and meditation as a nun.

The possibility that I was being called to be a nun worried me because I didn't and don't have any desire to cut myself off from people. I had spent years covering my ears when I was in the Catholic boarding school so that I wouldn't get the call from

God. The nuns thought we should hope and pray for this call every night before we went to sleep. As an adult, I was even surer I didn't want it. The thought of being asked to do something I didn't want to do tormented me. It became so intense that, at times, I doubted my own sanity. I was frightened by the entire experience to the point of asking myself: *Do I really want the peace and calm state of mind I have*? If so, on what is it conditional? Believing I was expected to give something back came very much from my Catholic upbringing. The notion that something this good could be given unconditionally – I just didn't believe it.

UNCERTAINTY OF THE UNKNOWN

"What lies before you and what lies behind you are unimportant compared to what lies within you."

~ Ralph Waldo Emerson

I continued to work as a volunteer at the mind, body, spirit organization in London, but left my job at the motorcycle firm because the guy who had triggered the Kundalini rising in the office had started dating another girl who worked with us. Seeing them together was too painful. I got a job as an editorial assistant for a medical journal. I was still pondering my future course spiritually when a guy at work invited me to a barbecue at his house. When I got there, everyone was sitting around, drinking and chatting. A box of what looked like homemade biscuits was offered to me, and I could tell that these were not normal biscuits. I think I knew that there was hash in them because they were offered as "cookies." I had never eaten one before, but was curious to see if it would affect my mind. Maybe I took it because I wanted to rise to the challenge – I didn't want my life to be as easy as it was.

Anyway, I ate one and about 20 minutes later, I was wracked with waves of paranoia. I thought everything and everyone was out to get me. I had never experienced such terror. Lying on a friend's bed with these waves rushing over me, I was filled with remorse for what I had done. I realized that there was a good chance that eating the cookie might have changed my state of mind. In those hours, I saw how stupid taking the drug had been. I couldn't shake the feeling that something was expected of me in return for the joy, serenity, and peace I enjoyed. Not knowing what it was, and the uncertainty this state created, messed with my mind after taking the drug. I wanted to turn the clock back, but of course, I couldn't. I had to accept the consequences of what I had done.

I returned home to sleep off the effects of the drug. When I woke again, I noticed a difference in my state of mind. The calm and serenity I had enjoyed for so long was gone. I was back to being the indecisive and highly-strung woman I had been before the first experience of Kundalini rising that morning in the office at work. I could feel my heart pounding through my chest. Later, I understood that they were palpitations. It was strange to hear my heart beating that way, and I kept thinking that its continuous and consistent beat was going to stop at any minute. My communication with people was strained once again. The ease I felt with others and they with me vanished. Indirectly and often directly, I had asked for this state to be taken away, and now my request was granted. Losing my connection to spiritual books and writings was most distressing. Once again, they were cold and sterile words on a page.

From my study of the Buddhist idea of attachment, I knew I shouldn't cling to the peace and serenity I'd been given. It was gone; I had to be grateful for the time I'd had it. I found it difficult to sing my heart out at my volunteer job for the mind-body center while expressing my gratitude for the time I'd experienced an altered state of consciousness. I felt sadness and loss; I was worried about the palpitations. Five days later, they stopped. My peaceful and calm state reemerged and life was once more in harmony and balance. Overjoyed and more grateful than ever that I had been given a second chance, I resolved that never again would I do anything to jeopardize this altered state of consciousness.

A couple of weeks after this experience, in July 1998, I participated in a seven-day meditation course called *Awakening the Heart* in Southern England. I felt a strong urge to extract myself from working life. I wanted to show my gratitude for the return of my altered state. I felt sorry for my lack of trust and was grateful for the opportunity the solitude would provide to do what I perceived to be the necessity of making amends to the universe.

This was my first retreat since returning from India, run along the same lines as the one in India —remaining silent except for *dharma* (wisdom) talks, question and answer periods, and small group sessions.

During the first meditation session, I realized my difficulty with sitting meditation had not disappeared. My calm state of mind didn't make this form of meditation any easier. No matter how hard I tried to focus on my breathing, my thoughts wandered. I was annoyed and frustrated. I had been given so much and yet I still couldn't focus. I couldn't watch the rising and falling of my breath without my mind wandering. It wasn't meant to be this way. Why couldn't I meditate? Why hadn't this change in consciousness affected my ability to meditate? Why did I still daydream my time away? I was still as bored and frustrated as ever. Lots of questions, but no answers. I don't know why I expected meditation to be easy.

Walking outside after that first session, I felt anger and a sense of helplessness about being unable to meditate. The periods of sitting meditation were still mental torture, as I battled with thoughts of not being good enough. I had been so hard on my mind, berating it for not being able to do something I believed should be easy — namely, being able to meditate. What I hadn't considered was how difficult meditation is. The mind has zero interest in meditating and will do everything it can to create a distraction.

The second day was no better. I resigned myself to a long week. Nevertheless, when I gave up fighting with my mind and just accepted that I was bored, a shift occurred, just as it had in India. When I accepted the boredom, I didn't feel as agitated. On the second day, we had the first small group session with one of the teachers, the opportunity to speak about what was happening in the meditation sessions. As the time allotted to each of us was short, I wracked my brain for something to say. Listening to others and hearing about the beautiful visual images they were having, and states they were reaching through meditation, was like being a visitor in another world. When it came to my turn, I just said, "I'm bored, the time goes so slowly when I do sitting meditation."

The teacher listened and nodded. She told me to be aware of these thoughts that came and went, and to accept them without trying to alter them. This was not what I wanted to hear. I wanted a technique that would make me able to meditate.

We had another group session on day three. This was a whole different experience. Not because of something the teacher or I said, but because of something another woman, whose first language was not English, said. She said how grateful she was for her mind and breath when she meditated, that it was like a friend who had come to her at birth, stayed with her all her life, and would leave her at death. Hearing this was like having a light turned on. I had heard similar things before and had read about the importance of being warm, welcoming, and gentle with myself during meditation. It's one thing to hear something or read it, and another to receive it. I really received it; the words hit at the deepest part of me and resonated. I saw clearly how my meditation had been fraught with dos and don'ts, instructions, orders, and damaging judgments, towards my mind and breath. A deep sense of shame came over me, and I had a mental image of my mind like a battered and bruised animal with the abuse that I had given it over many years. I resolved to be gentle during the next sitting.

I entered into the next meditation in a different frame of mind. I was gentle with my mind and breathing in a way I had never before attempted. I felt a tingling in my body, something completely new, a current of energy running through me, keeping me still. Then I experienced what I can only describe as orgasmic waves washing over me, bringing intense and exquisite pleasure. Without fear, I stayed connected to what was happening and, with every wave that rippled through me, connected fully with it. I was amazed that such experiences were possible from a peaceful process like meditation. When the bell went off to signify the end of the session, I forced myself to come out of it. I couldn't believe that I hadn't looked at my watch, not even once. I noticed that I felt spaced out and quite disorientated after it, but didn't want to speak to anyone because I felt my words would be ecstatic gibberish, as if there were no words to express what had happened and anything I said would be inadequate. Besides, it was a silent retreat.

I was thirsty and drank two full glasses of water before going out into the brilliant sunshine to continue with a period of walking meditation. Ambling under the sun, I pondered my first emergence into a proper meditative state and gave thanks.

Perhaps this experience meant that the remaining sittings would be free from boredom. I couldn't have hoped for anything better.

I went into the next sitting with a mixture of excitement and apprehension. I settled myself on my stool, pulled the blanket around my shoulders, and waited. In my previous meditations, I was ignorant about the possibilities and, therefore, had no expectations. But now my being had a metabolic-memory imprint of an experience and I wanted it to repeat. My agitation now was not from boredom, but from wanting and anticipating.

I didn't have to anticipate too long before the familiar tingle and waves of energy came over me again. I was filled with awe at the hidden wonders of the body and allowed myself to give into them for the duration. When the bell went off, I forced myself out of the meditation and felt spaced out and light-headed again. I drank a lot of water. The same story for days four and five. At night, I would hug myself and think that I was finally able to meditate properly and understand what it was all about.

I was concerned, though, about how spaced out and ungrounded I felt after each sitting. I felt that something wasn't quite right, although I didn't know what it was. I worried that I was becoming too attached to the pleasure it was giving me and that I was in danger of becoming a meditation junkie. I don't know why I thought this because I always forced myself to open my eyes the minute I heard the bell at the end of the session.

One night, I went to bed as usual and woke up at 3:00 AM to use the toilet. When I returned to the dormitory I was sharing with two other women, my inner voice told me to go to the meditation hall. My reaction was to laugh. It was 3:00 AM and I didn't want to go, but the voice persisted. I resisted it, tossing and turning in bed. And then, as if to encourage my complying, the two women in the other beds began to snore, not together, but one taking up when the other left off. Not having earplugs, I resigned myself to the inevitable. I put on my dressing gown and slippers and padded off to the meditation hall which luckily wasn't too far from the dormitory. Once in the hall, I settled myself on my stool and covered my shoulders with a blanket. I had the defiant thought: *Right, I'm here. Now what?*

I began to meditate and again, the tingling and pleasurable waves were not long in coming. I remained there for an hour or so — noticing that when able to end the meditation in my own time by allowing a wave or vibration to slow down naturally, instead of forcing the movements to end as I had done, I wasn't spaced out or disorientated. Somehow, the abrupt ending of the meditation by the bell upset a natural rhythm. I understood that now. I also knew why I had to go to the meditation hall on my own at 3:00 AM — to teach myself to follow my own pattern and not be constrained by a bell. Delighted and thankful at being given this lesson, I returned to a quiet dormitory and slept soundly until the bell awakened me for morning meditation. After this, I ended my sessions when it felt right for me. This usually wasn't long after the bell and there was no more disorientation or feelings of being spaced out. My fears about becoming a meditation junkie disappeared.

The next day, I settled down to meditate in my usual way. The waves changed into a kind of vibration that lifted me up. It was slow and gentle at first. My body wasn't lifted up physically because I always meditated with my legs wrapped around the stool, but I definitely felt a sensation of being lifted. With each energetic wave, I felt myself rising higher, the vibration rising and falling of its own accord. It would then fall, only to rise again immediately. There were times when the sensation of being lifted so high by the energy was such that I thought, *I am going to topple over and make a fool of myself in front of everyone.*

I resisted the vibration as strongly as I could until I couldn't fight it any longer. I thought, *That's it. If I make a fool of myself that's what I do, but I can't resist anymore.*

At this point, the vibration died down, but immediately began again, higher and higher. Then, always at a point I thought I couldn't bear any longer, it died down, only to begin again immediately. Not only did it lift me, it also began to rock me. I was being raised and rocked by energy. Strange as this experience was and at times, frightening, all of my Buddhist training taught me the importance of staying connected to whatever was happening, that there is nothing in the inner metaphysical world to be afraid of, so this is what I did. I could have opened my eyes at any time and ended the experience, but I chose not to. I was grateful that the precursor to these sensations was the gentle, pleasurable waves that had prepared me for this more intense experience.

On and on went the vibrations, bringing me higher and higher, and rocking me harder and harder. At every point, when I thought I was going to fall, the vibration would die, only to be replaced by a stronger and harder one. As the energy currents became more intense, I had an insight that resisting until the end — when it would recede of its own accord — was somehow not right. Instead of fighting this energy, I had to surrender to it. On the next wave that lifted me to a peak and rocked me, I said, "I surrender."

Immediately the current died. Relieved, I thought that this was the end. But to my complete amazement, it began again. This went on for many more vibrations. I was confused. I had surrendered to the energy. Why was it still happening? The meditation session ended, but I had no answer.

At the next small group session, I decided to speak about what was happening in my sitting meditations. I waited my turn and then gave a brief summary of what I was experiencing and asked what it meant and how to deal with it. I could tell from the teacher's response that she didn't have the slightest clue what I was talking about, but confirmed that my decision to keep my legs wrapped around the stool to keep myself grounded was the right thing to do. Deflated that I hadn't gotten either an explanation of what was happening or advice on what to do, I felt a deep isolation and realized that this was something I had to deal with on my own.

I approached the next sitting session more with fear and apprehension than excitement. The experience was not frightening when I was going through it, but it was afterwards when I had time to analyze it. I was determined to see it through to the end. I began to meditate. The session began as usual with the tingling of energy and then the vibrations began; up and up, higher and higher, rocking me forwards and backwards, strongly, faster and more violently. Each time I said "I surrender," they died down only to begin again with even more speed and intensity. I have no idea whether or not my body was physically rocking, but I knew that I wasn't being lifted up physically because I had my feet firmly locked around my stool. I experienced a moment of fear because although Buddhism had taught me about surrendering, that it was key and I was doing it, the experience wasn't ending – why?

Then, I knew. I don't know where the clarity or insight came from, but I knew what I had to do. I waited for the next vibration and without any fear and in complete surrender, unwrapped my feet from around the stool and said: "I surrender, but only to the light."

I didn't know what I meant by "the light." I don't remember seeing any lights, but I knew that I had to surrender completely, voluntarily, and with all of my being. That vibration ended and that was the last time I experienced similar rising energy currents for the rest of the retreat.

When I freed my feet from the stool and surrendered, I had no idea of what I was *letting go of.* I was in the grip of something that was not frightening, just utterly absorbing. One thing was clear: I couldn't have surrendered to nothingness. Somehow I knew that there was something *to surrender to.* During the remaining sitting sessions, the vibrations were much gentler and didn't lift or rock me at all.

My sense of freedom and elation when the retreat was over was indescribable. I felt that something deep and profound had happened, but didn't know what. Having come out of it on my own, I decided to keep it a secret and didn't speak to any of my teachers. The last thing I wanted to do was to speak and run the risk of being denigrated or confused about what had happened. I remembered the old spiritual saying, "Those who know don't speak and those who speak, don't know." So, for many years, I kept silent about this experience.

I returned to London feeling renewed and refreshed. I still didn't understand this energy that lies deep within the body. But it no longer concerned me. I was content to enjoy the experience and its benefits. I noticed I was receiving insights of my own. One morning, I was lying in bed and had an insight. We are all connected; it is but our perception that defines us as different. This creates the fear of separation and the thinking that everyone must fend for themselves as individuals. If we could see how we are all connected, there would be harmony and happiness in the world. Up to this point, I only had an intuitive understanding of what others described as "being and connectedness," now my own insights were emerging. I realized I could take these truths and develop them further. This amazed me. I was filled with even deeper gratitude for the gift of grace I had been given.

I also noticed that I began to breathe from my stomach. From my years practicing yoga, I learned about three-level breathing and how the deepest and most nourishing breathing is that which comes from the stomach. There were other physical changes, such as losing weight. I noticed these, but didn't think too deeply about them. What I was most conscious of was the speed with which insights and intuitions came. Insights like we *are not* our thoughts and feelings; we *have* thoughts and feelings but they are *not who we are*. After such an insight, I would feel the most incredible calm and contentment.

Although I had these wonderful shifts in understanding, I wanted to take on more study, but I didn't know what. I had been told I was a good tarot reader and had done a little when I was younger, so reading the cards seemed appealing. I decided to become a professional reader. But I couldn't without investing something in it — as I had never been properly trained in how to do readings. I found a teacher and every Monday evening for fifteen evenings, I went to his house.

For one hour, he taught me the meaning of each card. I did readings for several of his friends and got good feedback. My plan was to set up a business from home reading tarot cards. The night I finished my training, I had a dream. I don't remember many of the details, but I know that I was being shown something in a box with a lid, but then the lid shut down so that I couldn't see what was in the box. I took this to mean that I was not meant to be a tarot card reader. I was a bit annoyed that this dream came after I finished my training and paid out the money. But I took the message seriously and never read the tarot cards professionally. Not having a flesh-and-blood teacher, I rely on messages that come to me from the universe. To some, this may seem like a crazy way to live life because it demands total trust and surrender to the universe. Nevertheless, I took the dream to be a message from the universe and adjusted my plans accordingly.

I continued to work as a volunteer for the mind, body, and spirit center in London. As a volunteer, I was privileged to hear many inspirational speakers. I was working there as usual one evening when I picked up a book and suddenly froze. I was reading a sentence that spoke about the phenomenon of energy rising up from the base of the spine. The energy was called Kundalini. When I read this, I was amazed and wondered, *Is this what happened to me?*

I read on, "This energy is spiritual and powerful. It needs to be handled carefully." I read about its effects and was confused (i.e., *flashes of past lives, explosion of oneness*). None of this had happened to me. Yet, what else could this surge of energy through my spine have been? I couldn't shake off the feeling it *wasn't* Kundalini. So, I resisted this conclusion; yet, at the same time, I was fascinated by the new information my meditation practice had revealed to me. Every book I read seemed to mention Kundalini. To my amazement, I found out that there was even a form of yoga dedicated to raising the Kundalini, called Kundalini Yoga or Sahaja Yoga.

QUESTIONING THE EXPLANATION

"The Kundalini energy is a fire that burns away the web separating the non-self from the Self."

~ Author

Now that I had an explanation, which seemed to fit 80 percent of my experience in that it was energy that came from the base of my spine. I started to think: *Why me?* I'm not a nun. I haven't spent 24 hours a day, totally dedicated to the spiritual path. There must be a logical reason for why it happened to me. I don't always feel comfortable with spiritual people and have often been frustrated at the lack of scientific rigor which *New Age* spirituality spawns. For weeks, I pondered on why this happened to me. Then one evening, walking home from work through the park, I suddenly remembered my lazy right eye and wondered whether it had played a part in it. Could it be that because the left brain was not working at full capacity the right brain was actively compensating and the trigger for this rising energy came at a particular stage in my right brain development? When I got home, I googled *right brain* and *spirituality* and came up with millions of references linking the two. Then I entered *Kundalini* and *right brain* and more references came up. I was convinced that I had found the answer.

This interpretation meant that the experience didn't happen to me because I was special; it happened because I have a lazy eye that does not stimulate the left side of the brain so the right side works harder to compensate. This is why I have found it easy to understand the writing of saints and sages. I remembered that if one kidney stops working, the other kidney takes over; but, because the two kidneys perform the same function, no difference is identified. The two sides of the brain perform different functions, therefore, if one side is being used to compensate the lack of capability of the other side, the combined abilities of both sides are bound to be affected. To wit, a person with each side intact has more total brainpower than a person with one deficient side and one fully functioning side. This made perfect sense to me. Now all I needed to do was to get a scientist to back up this theory.

I wrote letters to psychologists and to ophthalmologists all over the world, outlining my theory and asking them for their views. A couple had the courtesy to reply to me, saying that sight from both eyes goes to both sides of the brain. Otherwise, the majority didn't bother to reply. I contacted a psychology professor who was in London for an international conference and he agreed to meet me in the evening after his conference. We went out for dinner and I explained all about my experiences and my theory.

He looked increasingly confused, until I talked about my "inner voice" and then he sat bolt upright and said, "Ah, you hear voices?"

I laughed and said, "Not like that." And he sat back again, dejected.

Eventually, he said, "You say all these things, yet you're not mad."

"No," I said, "just desperate for someone to believe me and support what I'm saying." He said that he couldn't help me, but asked me to stay in touch.

At this stage, I became frustrated and angry that something that made so much sense to me was proving so difficult for anyone else to understand.

I had talked to friends about my right brain and they joked about it. "Which side of the brain are you bringing out tonight?" they would ask. I laughed with them, but deep down I despaired. Would I ever find anyone to take me seriously? One night I was out with friends. We were talking about the link between the eye and the brain and a guy that I hadn't met before said: "Gordon Brown has a glass eye for his left eye."

I was euphoric when I heard this. *If Gordon Brown has a glass prosthetic for his left eye that might mean that his right brain is not being stimulated, which means that the left is working harder and so is it any coincidence that he had been Chancellor of the Exchequer of England?* I argued that this was the most left-brained job there is, having so much to do with mathematics and economics. This information inspired me and, as a result, I tried even harder to get someone to listen to me. I'm aware that one example doesn't add up to scientific proof, but this meager support for my theory satisfied me for the moment.

Would this energy have risen if I had two properly functioning eyes? The truth is I don't know; I don't think it would. I didn't consider myself particularly spiritual. I drank alcohol, enjoyed life, and could be hurtful to people. No, there had to be another reason why this had happened to me. In some way, I was accessing more right-brain energy than others. At a certain point, the additional right brain activity caused the Kundalini energy at the base of the spine to rise. If I could discover what the trigger was within the brain, then perhaps I could help people achieve the same peace, calm, and inner joy. This had always been my motive. I saw it as part of the vow I had made to be a Bodhisattva the night I had first heard about the concept in 1988 after attending my first Buddhist class.

In the meantime, I was reading everything I could get my hands on about Kundalini. I came across the work of an Indian man who has written extensively on the subject and I contacted him, telling him about my experiences and asking him about the influence of the right brain on Kundalini rising. He wrote back with advice and sent me some photocopied material from his other books. I was grateful and relieved that I had finally found someone who would listen to me. We became friends and I did some editing work for him. I wanted to get something published on the right brain and Kundalini, but didn't know how. When my Indian friend asked me if I would edit another book he was working on, I agreed on the condition that he would write a paper with me explaining my right brain theory. To my surprise, he agreed and in July 2002, we wrote *Kundalini, Soul and the Right Side of the Brain* that was published in *The Journal of Religion and Psychical Research* (Volume 25, Number 3, July 2002). I was delighted and had a sense of completing something that was important. I waited for the flood of letters and emails that I was sure would come from such a controversial article, but there wasn't even one comment.

After the article was published, I settled down and put my right brain development theory aside. I had done my bit by getting an article out in the world and no longer felt any urgency to do more. I started editing a book on *Shaktipat* for my Indian friend. Shaktipat is the ancient art of guru initiation practiced in the East where a guru with a look or a touch awakens the dormant Kundalini. It led to many heated debates as I discussed with him the need to have a guru. Like many Westerners, I wasn't happy with the idea of a guru. I remember once he said, "Achieving Enlightenment is not possible without surrendering to a guru."

Unnerved, yet adamant I said "We give away our power when we surrender to a guru. I am my own guru; I have all the answers within me."

He said, "That is what your ego mind wants you to believe so that it remains in control. Being your own guru in the way you believe is like the ego turning detective to catch a thief, which is itself; it's futile. You have to surrender to a guru who is outside the ego mind."

"But how do you recognize a true guru?" I asked. "Look at all the gurus who became corrupted after coming to the West. They became ego-inflated and caused much harm to their devotees."

I was aware as I was saying this that I was thinking about my past teacher who had abused his power in the Buddhist organization I was part of years ago. I was still angry about it.

Many times my friend tried to tell me that I didn't listen, that I thought I knew everything. But I thought he was trying to control me and I didn't like that.

I also didn't feel comfortable that he worked to raise the Kundalini of others. My experience with the energy had been seamless in that I had not experienced any adverse effects. I had a deep respect for the process and was horrified that anyone would try to raise it without knowing about an individual's somatic and metabolic state. To fully integrate the effects of this energy, you must have a strong nervous system, which is only achieved by a practice of spiritual preparation. I don't understand why I felt so strongly about this because when an experience is problem-free, it is usually shared without reservation. I recognized how powerful it is. Was it intuition that rendered me so concerned about the possibility of misuse by those setting out to intentionally raise Kundalini before the brain and body were sufficiently prepared to support it? I don't know, but something made me cautious.

Many books have been written on Kundalini rising prematurely. It is often called *spiritual emergency.* Stanislav and Christina Grof have written extensively about it. Two of the most authoritative writers on the subject, Gopi Krishna and BS Goel, had firsthand experience of a premature Kundalini activation and wrote about how it affected them throughout their lives. The first book I read following my discovery of Kundalini was Gopi Krishna's *Living with Kundalini.* The importance he placed on respecting and not messing around with this energy convinced me of its power. JJ Semple's experience as described in *Deciphering the Golden Flower One Secret at a Time* offers many parallels with my own, from his early experiences in boarding schools, his work in figuring out the role of sexual sublimation, and especially his theories of symmetry. He, too, urges following traditional meditation methods.

I had just finished editing the book on Shaktipat for my Indian friend when I remembered the man I had met in Varanasi six years earlier during my trip to track the life of the Buddha. He had given me a barrel covered with red cloth and had looked intently into my eyes and told me that life would get better. I wondered whether he had given me a Shaktipat initiation with his eyes — whether it was possible that he had raised my Kundalini. I had kept the red clothed barrel until a couple of days before I had this memory. Then I had thrown it out thinking, *I don't need to keep this anymore.* If I had known what it was, I would never have thrown it out. I have since learned that it was a Talisman, an object carried for protection. I linked my experience to what he had done for me and was overcome with gratitude. Then I remembered how he wouldn't take any money, only a donation. From then on, I could think of nothing else but returning to India to find this man and thank him.

THE IMPORTANCE OF GRATITUDE

"There is only one truth but an infinite number of ways of expressing that truth."

~ Author

I rummaged around in the box containing my photos from India and found the picture of the man in Varanasi. Looking at it, I felt a great sense of anticipation. I booked a two-week holiday in India and was excited at the thought of seeing him again. A week before I was due to fly, my dad became ill and was taken to hospital. I was faced with the toughest dilemma of my life. Do I cancel a promise I made to find and thank the man, or do I cancel my trip to be close to my Dad in case anything happens? I didn't know what to do. For the first time in my life, I humbly asked the universe for a sign to show me what it was I should do. I was passing by a house where some friends lived and I thought, *I'll drop in and tell them that Dad's in hospital.* When I rang the bell, they were delighted to see me and invited me into the sitting room. On the coffee table was a newspaper. I think it was the *Daily Mail*, folded in half, and the first word I saw in big black letters was 'INDIA.' It was about British Telecom setting up call centers in India. Filled with gratitude, I knew that I would go to India and nothing would happen to my dad while I was away. To many readers, this approach to deciding a course of action may seem baffling and somewhat arbitrary; but, for me, intuition has always been more reliable than intellect. My spiritual journey is all about trusting in a force that has my best interests at heart and letting go.

I arrived in Delhi in February 2003. I must have looked like I had some idea of where I was going. At least, I didn't have the pure tourist, *I don't have a clue* look. Walking down the street, a guy on a motorbike called out: "Welcome, second time to Delhi." This man and others like him spend their days watching tourists. He could tell I was familiar with the city.

I was keen to get out of there and get to Varanasi as soon as I could. I was worried about Dad, who was still in hospital. My family didn't understand why I hadn't cancelled the trip. If it had been an ordinary trip, I would have done so, without hesitation. But to me, this was a trip to give thanks. It had to be done. My mind was in terrible turmoil. I wanted to find this man and get back on a plane but, of course, I couldn't because it was a two-week holiday.

Once I'd registered in my hotel in Varanasi, I took the photo together with a "thank you" card and some dollars, and went out onto the streets. I showed the picture to many people. No one recognized him, until one man said, "I know this man."

"Will you take me to him?" I asked.

He agreed and also got very excited. We walked through familiar — yet not so familiar — dirty, crowded streets until I recognized the street where I had stayed before. My heart sank when we got to his house and although the door was open, he was not there. Fearing that I would not be able to find the way again if I left, and determined to finish what I had started, I said I would wait for him to return. I think word must have got out that a tourist was looking for him. After an hour, he returned, out of breath and quite agitated. He looked different than his photo and I immediately felt foolish. What was I doing here? I didn't know what to say, and he made no attempt to hide his irritation. Slowly, I tried to explain that I had seen him six years ago and asked, "Do you remember me?"

"I see lots of tourists," he snapped.

Fighting back my disappointment, I continued. "You said that life would improve for me and you gave me an object that you wouldn't take any money for, so I've come back to tell you that life has improved and to thank you for what you did." I handed him the thank you card. He took it and put it in his pocket without opening it. Then he stood up quickly.

"I'm glad that life is working out for you, now go," he said.

I don't know what I expected, but it wasn't being treated so abruptly. Fighting back tears and berating myself for having been so stupid to do this when my dad was in hospital, I went back to the hotel, exhausted. I wondered why he was in such a hurry for me to go. Unlike most Indians, he didn't add, "Tell all your friends that you have benefited and send them to me." There was no hype at all, which baffled me.

The rest of the time in Varanasi seemed long. I was in such emotional turmoil. I rang home regularly. Dad was still in hospital, but getting better. I willed the rest of the time to go quickly so I could return to London. On my 40th birthday, I abandoned my search for a rational explanation to account for my Kundalini experience. I took on the view that the energy had risen because of the spiritual practice I had been doing and/ or past karma. It had nothing to do with my brain. I did this in response to people who kept telling me that if I didn't stop looking for a scientific explanation, I would lose the gifts of peace and calm I had been given.

Having embraced Kundalini as *mine*, I read in *Mysticism*, by Evelyn Underhill, that it marks the beginning of the spiritual path of the mystic. I read everything I could about the mystical path and all of its stages. I was convinced that I was now on a *bona fide* spiritual path. I read so much because I wanted to know all about this path so that I could situate myself as to which of the various stages I was in.

I'm not going to be caught out, I thought. *I will know exactly where I am.* I thought I was one step ahead on the spiritual path.

It was the worst kind of arrogance: *spiritual.* This ego-inflation had me constructing visions of myself as a mystic. I became so sure that I was not only going to reach my goal of being a *bodhisattva,* but show everyone the way out of suffering. None of this was out in the open. They were ideas I held within.

In public, I was always warning about the dangers of the spiritual ego to anyone who would listen. But at home on my own, poring over books like *Mysticism*, I hugged myself thinking, *this is me.* All the while, my ego-inflation was growing. However, there are two qualities I have not let go of: humility and gratitude. Although the ego was growing, the humility by which I always thought *I've got these gifts through the back door without years of meditation and spiritual practice* was never far from my mind. I have always maintained an appreciation for every moment of every day, which has helped me come through.

WHEN THE BUBBLE BURSTS

"A true spiritual teacher is not the one who has the most students but the one who creates the most leaders."

~ Yogi Bhajan

Even though life flowed and was in balance, something was wrong. I was comfort-eating regularly and intensely, and I was frustrated and angry with myself. At the time, I believed spiritual people didn't have addictions, that they were exempt. My having this compulsion meant that something was wrong with me. I was spiritual, yet I had this behavior that I could not control. Once the craving struck, it was much stronger than I was, even worse when I went home to Ireland. Mum had to hide all the sweet things because I wouldn't stop until I had eaten everything. It wasn't greed; it was an overpowering need for fulfillment that brought me to the depths of despair.

To discipline myself not to comfort-eat, I set to studying intensively all the books on mysticism I could find. I learned about the dark night of the soul and recognized it as what I had just come through. I was feeling very sanctimonious and pleased with myself.

After a few weeks, I became a recluse, rejecting all contact with people. In a crowd, I felt alone and, although I never outwardly admitted it, I began to feel superior, as if my experience set me apart from others. I lost enthusiasm for everything except the spiritual books I bought and read quickly. Boyfriends and relationships were out of the question. I was on the path of the bodhisattva and nothing or nobody was going to get in my way.

If a guy tried to chat to me, I would be rude and distant. That is, until I let my guard down once again with a guy who was younger than I. Similar to my relationship with the young guy who had triggered the first rising of Kundalini in the office, this guy and I became friends. There was a link between us because he had studied philosophy at university. Unlike me, though, he was an atheist and had a logical and rational explanation for everything. I told him about my experiences, including those that involved taking drugs.

"Why do you think it's Kundalini?" he asked. This brought all my fears about labeling the experience as "Kundalini" into sharp focus.

"It's the only explanation I have found to account for what happened," I answered honestly. To this, he was quiet.

One evening, we arranged to go to the cinema. Beforehand, we went for something to eat. I sensed immediately that he was in a strange mood. We sat down and ordered.

"You don't get it, do you?" he blurted out of the blue.

"Get what?" I asked, confused.

"Get that the experience you had on that retreat was caused by the drugs you had taken two weeks earlier." I just looked at him, speechless, and not understanding what I was hearing. He continued.

"You haven't taken drugs since then, have you?"

"No" I replied."

"And you've had no more experiences like that?"

"No" I replied, again.

He then told me that the change of environment, food and intense meditation that a retreat provides meant that the extreme conditions activated again whatever was left of the drug in my brain. By this time, my mind didn't want to hear this, so it shut down. I started to argue with him but he got so frustrated, he stormed off.

"It's no good, I just can't get through to you," I heard him saying.

I went home. The next morning the first thing that came into my head was *drugs*. Had I had this experience because I took a hash cookie? Until then, even though I had written about this experience and about taking drugs on my website, nobody had connected the Kundalini with drugs. I certainly hadn't made the connection for myself. I had spent four years cutting myself off, pretending to myself that I was on a spiritual path. But now I was finding out it was drug-induced. I was in hell. All of a sudden, my entire world collapsed. I didn't know where to turn. I sank into a deep depression and was barely able to work. I went to my GP and said that I wanted an antidepressant, because I had had a shock, but didn't elaborate. She asked me if I was suicidal. I gave a wry smile.

"God doesn't want me," I said.

And that's what it felt like, that I had been kicked good and properly out of the spiritual world. She looked alarmed at this, but I reassured her by telling her it was a joke. She didn't know what to make of it all and hastily scribbled down the prescription. She said she would increase it if there was no change. Clutching the piece of paper, I went to the chemist and got my pills. This was my only lifeline. Whatever was wrong with me, it wasn't spiritual. I was suffering from depression, it had nothing to do with the "dark night" or anything else spiritual. I couldn't look at spiritual books. I felt like they were all laughing at me. I was as alone as anyone can be. Once the antidepressants kicked in, they were marvelous. They confirmed to me that I had never been on a spiritual path. If I had been, they wouldn't have had the effect that they did — and what an effect!

I hadn't felt like this during the years I had been closeted with my books. I had energy and enthusiasm for life and people; I looked and felt better than I had in ages. Moreover, I was relieved at not having to carry the burden of becoming a bodhisattva, having to save the world according to the scenario my imagination had concocted. Minus the weight that goal had placed on me, I didn't feel the pressure anymore.

I went out and enjoyed life. However, at the same time, something strange was happening. I wanted to be comfortable around people and them around me, but this wasn't happening. I felt isolated, cut off, and unable to connect, which was scary because I was trying to get back to a world I'd left many years ago — but the way was blocked. I couldn't go back to the spiritual, so where was I? Nowhere. This had to be hell.

One Saturday night I was sitting in my flat, in absolute misery. The light dose of antidepressants had lost their effect, and I was once more plunged into the deepest despair. I thought back to earlier years when my inner voice told me to give up everything spiritual. And I had done it. Why wasn't I able to continue a different life? Instead, I thought that I had been invited to pursue the mystical path. I was angry at what I believed was God or the universe playing games with me. I wanted to get back to the world I had left, but couldn't. Could I find a way out of no way?

A Cycle Completed

"The journey to Self does not end. What ends are cycles on that journey."

~ Author

Alone and lonely that night, my inner voice spoke three words: *do a course*! I marveled at this because four years earlier, somebody had recommended I do a self-development course in London.

Without a teacher, I had always taken third party messages from the universe seriously, so I went to an introductory evening, which I found hyped and full of marketing. I walked out after an hour, dropping a derogatory comment to the guy on the door about everyone there being mad. Now, four years later, I remembered it. In the intervening four years, I hadn't thought about it or met anyone who talked to me about it.

The next day, I called the Landmark office in London to ask when their next Landmark Forum weekend was taking place; they told me September. I registered for that weekend and found it to be a powerful experience. That weekend completed what I had started, but couldn't finish. I had spent most of my life developing self-awareness, so it was ironic that I learned more about myself over that weekend than in all my years studying Buddhism and practicing meditation. This is not to dismiss the time I spent practicing Buddhism. It was the preparation during those years that made the Landmark Forum so powerful because what I had heretofore only known in theory became real. The Forum made it real by relating it to certain events in my life I had repressed. The weekend forced me to examine events in my life that I had never looked at. I thought that the spiritual was all about looking forward and not living in the past. Going for the goal of enlightenment did not involve the past so I never went there because of the pain it brought to the surface. What I realize now is that the *spiritual* cannot be used as a plaster to mask pain. There can be nothing false on this path and my not dealing with the effects of certain events in my life had caused me to become stuck spiritually. I was using energy to shield myself from the effect of emotional pain. To make progress, I had to free this energy.

Over three days of the Landmark Forum, I saw how I had created a story for everything that happened to me and how I ran my life, based on an assumption that the story was true.

My mother had shouted at me when I was five. The event was real in that she did shout at me, but what I made it mean, my made-up story (i.e, that she didn't love me and that I was unlovable) was my invention. I believed it to be true and had been living my life based on the constructs of a deluded, peevish five-year-old. Realizing this was both funny and liberating, it transformed the way I looked at myself and at life. Transformation and power come when we have the insight and the courage to separate our story about what happened from what actually happened. When we do this, life flows and it becomes the magical experience it is meant to be. Landmark Worldwide teaches how the human being is put together, how he/she is designed. With this knowledge, it is possible to look at the design and, given who and what we want to be in the world, decide whether or not it serves us. If it doesn't, then it's possible to create a new design that serves our goals.

I remembered the incident with the nun and how she told me that I was functioning at borderline mental handicap. With penetrating clarity, I saw that it wasn't what she said that had such an impact, but the interpretation I put on what she said. I made "borderline mental handicap" mean that I would never amount to anything, and I saw how this story had impacted everything in my life. With understanding came tremendous relief, and I realized what I had made it mean was only my invention. It wasn't true; and, because it wasn't true, I could let it go. How different my life might have been if I'd made what she said mean *I was a genius* and had based my self-image on this premise.

In that instant, I felt the impact of the disempowering story I had made up about my life. It had subtly dominated my life up to that point. When I saw this, I felt great relief and knew that I had resolved an issue that had been playing at the back of my mind. Closure meant I could let it go and move on with my life without feeling any bitterness toward the nun who had said it.

Landmark education and training enables power, freedom, and full self-expression by invoking possibility, which is a way of being. What I learned from the weekend was *who I think I am* is not *who I really am*. It is the way of being I'd put in place as an unhappy five-year-old. That weekend I got a glimpse of who I really am, which is whoever or whatever I choose to be. This insight was so liberating it left me breathless. I didn't have to be the way I had been. I had a choice to create a new way to be in the world.

From the beginning of the weekend, I saw many parallels between the Eastern idea of transcending the ego and what Landmark achieves in unraveling what we think of as our identity. Landmark explains that one of the ways it achieves results is through a "technology" based on the mechanisms of integrity and authenticity, a program that aims to achieve complete self-awareness through taking responsibility for areas in life over which we haven't been honest in our dealings with others or ourselves. The minute we admit we haven't been honest, the possibility for honesty and authenticity is created.

The Forum consists of three days during which the participants painfully and movingly engage in this process. People got up to share and in every shared declaration, I could see something of myself. I realized that I was no different from anyone else. I am human, and while my stories are different, they share commonality with everyone else's, as they are only stories. The truth of our interconnection went way beyond books and words. Even though I thought I was aware of the power and seduction of the ego, I considered myself superior to everyone because of the spiritual experiences I had. I believed I knew what was best for everyone, including myself. The irony is that I had warned lots of people about ego inflation just because I had been on a path traveled by only a few. Seeing this was liberating, and I smiled wryly at just how deluded I had been. There is a game being played: to arrive at a non-ego state and in that moment to realize the Self that remains when everything that is *not-Self* falls away.

At the end of the weekend, I knew intuitively that human beings suffer because past decisions influence their thoughts and actions. Freedom comes from identifying these decisions and putting them back in the past, which leaves the future as a blank canvas, primed and ready for something to fill it. It freed up the energy for me to continue on my spiritual path with integrity.

I resolved to work tirelessly within this structure to give human beings the tools by which they can free themselves from their own suffering. I saw Landmark technology as a vehicle for fulfilling the bodhisattva vow I made in 1988. I must stress that this is my personal choice and not something that Landmark Worldwide has endorsed. Human beings suffer; the Buddha said this. The vow I made when I first heard the concept of the bodhisattva was that if I was ever worthy enough to learn the cause of human suffering, and have the tools to relieve it, that I would work tirelessly to do so.

From my own experience, I realized that our identity/personality/ego — call it what you will — is nothing more than the sum of decisions we have made up about who we are and how life is. They cause us to suffer because these decisions, though past, still operate on our lives as if they were real and, hence, create what Buddhists call the world of Maya, or the unreal world — the world of illusion and delusion.

I look at Landmark as a spiritual program, which is how it unfolded for me. It's not everyone else; that's not possible. We all see things differently. I believe the Landmark Forum takes a person from the *hall of ignorance* through to the *hall of learning*. I'm not sure if it takes one into the *hall of wisdom* because the education is an ontological study that looks solely at how human beings are put together, identifying what makes us human, but doesn't go much beyond that except for filling the *nothing* space with possibility. I believe that what happens in the hall of wisdom is more profound, but the foundational work of the Landmark Forum is in finding a way through the halls of ignorance and learning. There are other self-development programs besides Landmark Worldwide. It was important for me to do some self-development training because, even on the spiritual path, undertaking it alone was difficult due to the chameleon-like nature of the mind and ego. The mind has no interest in bringing about the profound shift of consciousness required for spiritual awakening. It is only interested in the information gathered by the senses since birth.

One distinction made during the Landmark Forum weekend that challenged me concerned *intuition*. I believe in intuition as an inner teacher. During the weekend, we were asked to consider the possibility that intuition is not a reliable test of reality. This was difficult for me because for many years, my intuition had been strong and accurate; and, I was reluctant to consider it in any other way. I listened to the arguments about intuition being unreliable (i.e., not based on objective evidence) and was prepared to be open about it. It was late in the day when we finished and I was rushing to get the last tube. I knew that one tube line ran longer than the others, but my intuition said the "District Line" was stronger. I fought against it for a bit, but then decided it had always worked for me and headed off towards that tube line. When I got to the station platform, a voice over the Tannoy said, *This is the last District Line of the evening, all other trains on other lines have stopped running.*

My heart swelled with love and gratitude when I heard this and I resolved not to give up on my intuition. Luckily, Landmark Education doesn't proclaim what it says to be the truth, but only requests that its ideas be considered. In this case, I pondered what was said about intuition and then respectfully not taken ownership of that idea. This followed my pattern of listening to what is said, but then going within to verify it against my own experience.

Having the freedom to do this is important on the spiritual path. Although the destination is the same for everyone, the journey — how we get there and what we do to get there — is different for everyone.

After completing the Landmark Forum I returned to the spiritual path and to reading spiritual books, but in a humbler frame of mind. Once again, I was at the beginning. This time I wouldn't pretend that I knew everything. Since that guy had pointed out the influence of the hash cookie to me, I'd had a nagging doubt about the spiritual/mystical experience. I couldn't say for sure that the experience was drug induced, nor could I say that it wasn't. This continued to haunt me because integrity and honesty are crucial when travelling the spiritual path.

In February 2007, I hosted an event for parents/caretakers of special needs' children and adults in West London. The event involved giving parents/caretakers 20 minutes of Reiki healing, free of charge, to acknowledge the important work they do. It was a *thank you* from me to the children and adults that I had worked with in Cregg House in Ireland who had given me so much.

I am trained as a Reiki healer and have experienced its power. The event went well. I was touched by how grateful those who received the healing were. At the end of the session, the Reiki healer refused to take any money for the voluntary time she had donated. As a way of giving her some money, I requested a healing session from her. I would be the client. She agreed and we set a date.

On the day, I was apprehensive and not at all sure why I was going. My inner voice went on a rant, throwing out various reasons for not going. Pushing these reservations aside, I decided to go. I lay down on my stomach on the table. Then the healing began. After a few moments, my right arm started to jerk, then my left and then suddenly an energy from the base of the spine started to course up through me, making me jerk and shudder in a fit-like manner. The healer was concerned and asked me to breathe deeply. When I did this, the jerking ceased, only to begin again intensely. Once again I connected to this experience without any fear. I had a memory of what was happening and I knew that all I had to do was surrender, which is what I did.

After the session, I felt incredibly cold, despite the day being quite hot for London. I could tell by the healer's reaction that she had never seen energy in the body behave like that before. She told me to drink plenty of water and to call her in a couple of days. The session was in my local gym and as I was going out, I met a friend who was working out. He was concerned about how I looked and asked if something was wrong. I tried to explain what had happened, which he dismissed by saying, "Oh, she hit a nerve."

I didn't have the energy to speak more with him, so I said goodbye and walked home. I was so tired I cancelled my plans to go out that evening. I went to bed early and to my amazement, my body started to convulse like it had earlier at the Reiki session. Once again, I surrendered to the energy, cooperating completely with what it wanted to do and where it wanted to take me. After a while, it subsided and I slept fitfully until morning.

When I woke up, I was relieved and euphoric. This experience of rising energy had occurred without any hint of a drug, and I realized that the profound experience I'd had on the meditation retreat in Devon was also not drug induced. But it had permanently shifted my consciousness. Why? Because *it is doing me*. I no longer have to think about "*Is it real?*" There's room for consciousness expanding realizations.

Since the Reiki session, I often experience energy rising and falling in my body, always just before sleeping. It varies in nature. Sometimes it's a shaking motion; other times I feel my body being moved in a circular direction. I always surrender to it and accept its will without fear. My insights are more frequent and come to me as fully formed pictures. I feel vindicated. I don't have "was it or wasn't it" questions about the drug hanging over my head. I have come to the end of a journey, but I am also beginning again, albeit older and wiser. The journey to self-knowledge does not end. What ends are the cycles on the journey. For me, one cycle has finished and a new one is beginning.

PART II

REFLECTIONS ON THE JOURNEY

THE CHAKRAS

"Kundalini led me to an intensive, transformative, self-development training. I was able to identify specific events in my life where the energy had become frozen."

~ Author

According to some mystics, every human being is composed of three energy bodies: the physical, subtle, and causal. Kundalini together with the three major *nadis,* or nerves, the *Sushumna, Ida,* and *Pingala,* along with the seven vortices of energies called chakras are located in the subtle energy body. The movement of Kundalini, while felt by the physical body, is actually happening in the subtle energy body.

Kundalini works by unblocking energy trapped largely in the first three chakras, the physical, emotional and mental during the first 21 years of life. If you clicked a shutter, freezing the energy in snapshots at each of these seven-year intervals, you'd see the energy trapped in these chakras at these points in time. At birth, the energy flows freely, but an event — which may or may not be associated with physical, emotional or mental trauma — can cause the energy to get stuck.

By the time we reach 21 years of age, the first three chakras can become blocked. The unblocking of the energy at these chakras unifies the physical, emotional, and mental, balancing the personality. There is a subtle energy web called the etheric, which separates the physical from the emotional and is burned away by the Kundalini, resulting in harmony between body and emotions.

So, how do we go about unblocking the energy in these chakras, and is it done before or after Kundalini rises? In my case, it happened after my Kundalini rose. Kundalini led me to an intensive, transformative, self-development training. I was able to identify specific events in my life where the energy had become frozen and, through summoning the courage to face these events, the energy was unblocked and released at a conscious level. For me, this was a process of becoming conscious of and taking responsibility for the decisions I made that froze the energy physically, emotionally, and mentally.

The longest period of my spiritual journey was the unblocking of energy in the first three chakras. After that, because of the relatively unimpaired status of the remaining four chakras, the energy traveled upwards and downwards with ease.

I taught Kundalini yoga because it allowed me to direct this energy intentionally, to clear out these blockages without the suddenness of a full-fledged Kundalini rising. Through a progressive practice like Kundalini yoga and a healthy lifestyle, the energy gets unblocked, safely and naturally. The individual becomes aware of the intended purpose associated with these chakras. For example:

- Feeling more secure and confident of one's place in the universe — the result of unblocked Kundalini energy in the first chakra,
- Identifying and controlling emotions that arise without feeling the need to act on them — the result of unblocked energy Kundalini in the second, emotional chakra,

As a consequence of working with Kundalini energy through yoga and meditation, shifts happen: worldview, emotional balance, and consciousness are expanded. Unless the groundwork of clearing out the blocked energy from the first three chakras is done, flights into altered states of consciousness are illusory. They are not permanent. Without clearage, all we can expect is a transitory glimpse of higher consciousness, a poor representation of the energy operating in the higher chakras. A glimpse can be unsettling, in terms of one's ability to feel grounded and stable in the here and now.

Perhaps it's because I teach the chakras in my weekly Kundalini yoga class that I've been thinking about all seven energy centers located in the subtle energy body. One week I focused on awakening the heart chakra, the fourth.

Prior to this class, I had taught the first three chakras — physical, emotional, and mental — and at some point had the realization that these chakras are very much concerned with instinct and survival. They also comprise what we think of as our identity, our personality, who I AM. Each chakra corresponds to the first seven years of life so, as you can imagine, by the age of 21, a lot has happened during our lives to cause energy to become frozen in these chakras. This is why the instruction "know yourself" is so critical to awakening.

"Know yourself," not "judge yourself," is an important distinction. When realization arrives, it is easy to get into blame or guilt. This is a trap.

Dealing with first realizations — when energy becomes unfrozen in the first three chakras — is also important. For example, when I first realized that the desire to disengage from the adult world had been motivating my spiritual journey, I was shocked, but also liberated. It enabled me to create an adult relationship with spirituality — one based on being in the world, not alienated from it, alone in an altered state of consciousness.

The process that freezes this energy is often unpleasant. It can take the form of dark thoughts and unfounded opinions, coupled with feelings of being unsettled and agitated without knowing why — at least that was how it was for me.

Because the process of spiritual awakening is not linear, there are still days when I'm prone to negativity. Staying with facts and not getting drawn in or absorbed by what is going on in the mind or body enables me to recenter myself.

Unfrozen or transformed energy in the first three chakras prepares the way for one of the most prodigious leaps in consciousness a human being can experience, the shift from the third chakra (solar plexus) to the fourth — the heart.

This shift marks the beginning of what it is to be a human being, the shift from "Me" to "We." The realization that there is no separation, just the illusion of separation, followed by the desire to make a difference, to make a contribution to the world — not based on ego, but one based on a genuine desire to act.

Wanting to make a contribution without any ego attachment defines this stage of awakening. At this stage, we realize we are not the mind/body, but that which watches everything that arises from the mind/body. It is the stage of deep compassion both for oneself and others. Everything is Love and, most importantly, that there is nothing wrong either with oneself or with life.

With the heart fully awakened, it becomes a matter of grace as to whether or not consciousness shifts and stimulates the final three chakras, which are relatively clear of blocked energy. However, whether or not consciousness awakens permanently to complete the individuation process occurs on a case-by-case basis.

QUALITIES OF SPIRITUAL AWAKENING

"There is the realization that 'the other' is me. Wakening at the level of identity or ego, there is the realization that I am not the body-mind, and it's a letting go."
~ Author

I have long pondered the nature of spiritual awakening and its qualities. When I have a thought about something, I use it like a Japanese koan. I think about it constantly, remaining alert and vigilant to anything I hear or read that validates what I have been pondering.

I have been wondering about the variety of spiritual awakening experiences and wondering if they are all the same. Intuitively, I feel they aren't, but I don't have any sources to corroborate my hypothesis. I do this because Truth IS absolute. If what I am thinking is in alignment with Truth, then I will find something to back it up; if I don't, then no matter how alluring the thought, I won't find anything, so I'll drop it.

A couple of weeks ago, I came across the writings and videos of an American living spiritual teacher called Adyashanti who has practiced Zen Buddhism for 15 years. As I watched his YouTube video, *Different Qualities of Awakening*, I sensed intuitively that he was spiritually awakened.

When my Kundalini rose 14 years ago, it transformed my identity, my egoistic state, and I became more and more self-aware of how my ego had been put together and how Kundalini has dismantled it. It is this transformation of identity that distinguishes spiritual awakening from the plethora of documented spiritual experiences.

When it affects the body, it triggers neurobiological cleansing and healing. When it affects the mind, it produces the well-documented experiences mystics describe: loss of boundaries, oneness or non-duality, an emergence into the absolute or formless realm. When Kundalini wakes the heart, there is the experience of heart opening — the interconnectedness and non-separation of everything, and an outpouring of love and compassion.

There is the realization that "the other" is me. Wakening at the level of identity or ego there is the realization that I am not the body-mind, and it's a letting go. This is the most challenging aspect of awakening because it demands a total giving up or letting go of the body-mind, which creates a huge amount of fear that must be faced. One can experience awakening at all three levels (body, mind, heart), but this is rare.

Awakening at the body level may only result in the inability to awaken the mind or heart.

Awakening at the level of mind usually results in the individual's withdrawing from the game of life and ultimately losing himself in the formless realm of the absolute. At some point, this spiritual honeymoon ends, precipitating a difficult reentry into everyday life.

Awakening at the heart level alone can be dangerous in that the heart becomes so open and connected that discernment — a vital ingredient, both before and after Kundalini rises — is missing. Hypersensitivity and being easily hurt are the hallmarks of an awakening at the level of heart only.

Given that the interest in higher consciousness is increasing across the world, it is likely that spiritual awakenings will happen much more frequently. It is important to map the types of spiritual awakenings and their effect on life after such awakenings.

A spiritual consciousness awakening at all three levels results in the experience of wisdom, love, and truth, but these are but a by-product of an awakening. What matters is what the newly awakened state of consciousness provides to the world. You already are what you seek.

I have been on a spiritual path since my teenage years. From early on, I knew there was a difference between being religious and being spiritual, and I chose the latter. I had no idea what it meant or might involve. It took the form of a search, mostly through Buddhism, which I studied and practiced for many years. Then I went to India. When I came back, I didn't know what to do next. I had gone as far as I could with Buddhism. Pondering this one morning in my flat, I had a strong intuition about "giving up everything." Because of my many years as a "searcher" and my comfort level reading spiritual books and attending spiritual conferences, this was the last thing I wanted to do.

The spiritual path is different from the religious path because there is no authority over the spiritual. You are your own authority, or more specifically, you must learn to recognize the still, small voice within; it is the only guide on the spiritual journey. So, when my still, small voice instructed me to give up everything, I listened. I have some reservations about referring to a "voice talking to me" because of the association with hearing voices being a particular form of mental illness, but I must remain true and authentic to what happened. So I listened, obeyed, and gave up the "search."

Then a few months later, I had the first of two experiences of energy rising from the base of the spine. This totally unexpected and unprepared (consciously) event turned my attention from things external to what lies within and that became my search. I now realize that searching for the source of an experience and getting hooked took me away from the real goal, which was the realization of self: THAT which was, prior to the "search."

I also realize that a "search" is only purification. My time spent studying and practicing Buddhism wasn't a search; it was purification of karma so I could take responsibility for everything that had happened to me. Training to teach Kundalini yoga was also a purification. The early morning intensive, eight-day retreat — starting the day at 3:30 AM and ending at 11:00 PM each night — wasn't a search; it was a purification. Purification included anything standing between me and the realization of That.

To see it as a search is to deny that we already are That, and there's stuff in the way that stops us from realizing That. Experiences are only pointers to That, they are not It. So to search, which is very much what the ego wants to do, only serves to maintain the illusion of separation. There is no separation. We are already That, which we are searching for, so all we need to do is watch how the mind wants to take us away from That. Ultimately, it is all so simple, which is why enlightenment has always and ever will be heralded by laughter...the ultimate joke... searching to be That, which we already are.

Kundalini provides the awareness that, once we learn to observe the inner landscape, this "witness mentality" gradually allows us to realize we are not separate from that which we seek.

An article in the *London Daily Telegraph* got me thinking. I have always claimed to be spiritual, not religious, and this article asserts that "spiritual people struggle to cope mentally more than religious people." The figures are quite dramatic — so-called spiritual people are 77 percent more likely than the others to be dependent on drugs, 72 percent more likely to suffer from a phobia, and 50 percent more likely to have a generalized anxiety.

The study was based on a survey of 7,403 randomly selected men and women in England who were questioned about their spiritual and religious beliefs, and their mental state. The researchers concluded that there is increasing evidence that people who profess spiritual beliefs in the absence of a religious framework are more vulnerable to mental disorder.

The article doesn't delve into the reasons why, which leaves the field open for me to offer my own conclusions.

Judging from my own experience, being spiritual is different than being religious in that there are no rules or rituals governing one's spiritual life. There is no cozy community of like-minded people, no conformist attitudes favoring group-think. Quite the opposite. The spiritual quest is a solitary endeavor, very much a path of the alone, by the alone, for the alone, with not very much light at times. To be spiritual is to turn your attention to what goes on within. It is a path of expanding self-awareness.

Why should this path pose a risk to mental health? One reason might be the kind of intense introversion that accompanies the spiritual quest and the various types of meditation. Although these hold the potential of awakening dormant energies in the body, activating these energies may result in the person's experiencing various hallucinations, either auditory, visually, or other. This is not limited solely to those claiming to be spiritual; it can happen as a result of intense trauma. A surge of this energy into the brain can alter consciousness, which can lead to mental health issues, if not managed correctly.

Religion doesn't carry the same risks. There isn't the same kind of experimentation taking place in the laboratory of the body. Religion is pretty much a passive affair — you attend, you listen, you're told what to believe. Yes, you do pray, often only halfheartedly, and without conviction.

Both Gopi Krishna and Isaac Bentov believed that the mentally ill were actually highly evolved, but were unable to deal with the material world and were, therefore, labeled mentally ill. Although they did not actively seek spiritual or mystical pursuits, the hidden energies that induce higher consciousness somehow came alive in them, confusing and incapacitating them, rendering them unfit by the social standards of everyday life. This may explain why certain individuals who are not spiritual seekers fall into melancholy, homelessness, mental illness, and/or poverty, and are powerless to do anything about it. According to Gopi Krishna and Issac Bentov, one aspect of their beings — could it be the right brain? — may evolve so suddenly that they become unable to cope with everyday life.

The spiritual quest engages all the senses, the mind and the body, too. It is an active undertaking. Not everyone is up to it. Yet, with the proliferation of trendy New Age fads, many unstable individuals dabble with pursuits they should probably avoid. The spiritual quest requires resilience, skepticism, and the ability to troubleshoot. If this sounds like the character qualifications for becoming an engineer, then you're on to what it takes. The spiritual quest is the reengineering of the Being. Only certain individuals succeed therein.

By focusing on rituals and dogma, religions cultivate a safe, social environment for their followers, one steeped in contradictions: They scorn the pursuit of wealth at the same time they drive themselves to amass it; they extol the simplicity of Jesus at the same time they themselves live lives of opulence. Resilience is unnecessary; skepticism is discouraged; troubleshooting is unheard of.

But while religion is safe, it doesn't produce the richness of mystical experience that Carl Jung once described: "He who looks outside, dreams; he who looks inside, awakens." So, while I have had to manage my mental health — to attain the richness I now have — I will always and forever take spiritual over religious. At the same time, I will always be aware of the challenges that spirituality creates.

NEUROSCIENCE AND THE SPIRITUAL

"I am no neuroscientist/neurosurgeon, so I can't comment on this. However, the description of the pain he endured and the associated physical symptoms screamed 'Kundalini' to me."
~ Author

Recently, I submitted a draft paper for my MSc in Consciousness, Spirituality, and Transpersonal Psychology to my personal tutor for comment before submitting the final paper. In his feedback, he wrote that it might be useful to look up the works of Eckhart Tolle, Byron Katie, and Dr. Eben Alexander. I am familiar with Eckhart's work, having read *The Power of Now* and *A New Earth* many times. I am less familiar with Katie, but I know the system she has developed called, The Work, which is based on questioning our thoughts and asking, "Is this thought true?" I haven't read any of her books or attended any of her trainings. However, I have heard both her and Tolle speak when I was a volunteer at a mind, body, spirit center in London some years ago.

However, I knew nothing about Dr. Eben Alexander. I hadn't even heard his name until my tutor mentioned it in his comments. All my tutor gave me was his name, so my first stop was Wikipedia, which I realize isn't the best academic source, but I wanted to get a general flavor of what he is claiming and what he is claiming shocked me. He is claiming nothing less than proof of heaven, which is the title of his book about his near death experience (NDE).

I have been ambivalent about reports of NDEs. I feel intuitively that they stem from brain activity — particularly right brain temporal lobe activity triggered by spontaneous Kundalini. However, the fact that this account was written by a well-respected neurosurgeon (Dr. Alexander), who knew a great deal about neuroscience, got me to thinking. If my tutor recommended this research and expected to see some reference to it in my final paper, I had better knuckle down and find out more about it.

On my way to work, I stopped off at a bookshop and asked if they had *Proof of Heaven: A Neurosurgeon's Journey into the Afterlife* in stock. I was in luck; the shop assistant took the last copy from the shelf. Glancing briefly at the cover I saw that the design included a butterfly, which holds personal significance for me. Feeling intuitively that there was something important in this book, I purchased it, thanked the shop assistant, and left.

When I returned home from work that evening, I opened the book and began to read. Dr. Alexander claims that e-coli bacterial meningitis shut off the neocortex of his brain, which resulted in his coma and subsequent NDE. I am no neuroscientist/neurosurgeon so I can't comment on this. However, the description of the pain he endured and the associated physical symptoms screamed "Kundalini" to me.

On page 13 of the book, he writes, "I shifted slightly in bed and a wave of pain shot down my spine." In the next paragraph, "Instantly the pain ratcheted up another notch — a dull, punishing throb penetrating deeply at the base of my spine." On page 16, he says: "Pushing open our bedroom door, she (Eben's wife) saw me lying in bed just as before. But looking closer she saw that my body wasn't as relaxed as it had been, but rigid as a board. She turned on the light and saw that I was jerking violently. My lower jaw was jutting forward unnaturally, and my eyes were open and rolling back in my head."

On pages 17-18, he continues: "When the EMTs wheeled me into the Major Bay 1 of the ER, I was still convulsing violently while intermittently groaning and flailing my arms and legs. They went to work on me, I was squirming like a six-foot fish pulled out of the water. I spouted bursts of garbled, nonsensical sounds and animal-like cries."

Reports of NDEs often feature a bright, but enveloping, benevolent light. I hold the Buddhist view that there is nothing in the inner world to be afraid of and while I haven't had the rich intense, vivid visual experiences Dr. Alexander had, the convulsions are something I identify with. For many weeks and months after raising Kundalini, my body would convulse just before sleeping. It still happens occasionally, but I have learned to trust and surrender to the energy and when the episode ends, I am left feeling calm and relaxed.

After reading his account, I googled Dr. Eben Alexander and kundalini to see if anyone had connected his experience to

Kundalini, but the combination only resulted in a few articles. Had I expanded my search to include near death experience and kundalini, I would have found many links. I am very aware that the connection between the two, although rather commonplace, has not been extensively explored. Nevertheless, those of us who are more experienced with this energy need to read Dr. Alexander's account, as well as the many other NDE accounts. If the consensus is that NDEs are driven by the spontaneous eruption of Kundalini energy, it solidifies the hypothesis for research around the connection between Kundalini and NDEs.

However, as interesting as his book is, I'm not sure his experience constitutes proof of heaven. He needs more time to assimilate his experience, more time to research it, more time to think about it in scientific terms before conferring a religious status on the states he passed through.

It would be useful to hear the accounts of those who treated him in the ER and know more about the drugs they administered. Will he dig deeper into the physical causes and the anatomical processes that induced the experience?

Has Dr. Alexander ever heard of Kundalini? And, if so, will he pursue the connection to NDE, specifically to his experience? Does he understand that both Kundalini and NDEs take time to integrate? It took Gopi Krishna 20 years before he was able to write about his Kundalini experience. JJ Semple needed almost 30 years to be able to write about his experience. Will Eben Alexander continue to write about his? Or is his first book a "one and done"?

At the Kundalini conference I organized and facilitated in April 2013, one of the speakers, a Kundalini Yoga Master, was asked the question, "Is Kundalini dangerous?" His reply was, "I think it is dangerous to ignore Kundalini."

Intuitively, I feel that Kundalini is the vehicle that is shifting certain people's consciousness. Why these people and not others, I don't know? Nevertheless, we should be aware of the relationship between Kundalini and the NDE. That the two phenomena share enough commonalities for us to conclude that they are related.

Perhaps Dr. Alexander's account is most notable because of his standing in the medical community as a respected neurosurgeon. Is he now considered a renegade because he ventured beyond the accepted confines of science? What do his colleagues think? He and his book have received a torrent of backlash from atheist neuroscientist, Sam Harris, who sees Dr. Alexander's book damaging the argument that consciousness is a by-product of the brain. Will Dr. Alexander recant?

As of this writing, it also appears he no longer agrees with the neo-atheist position. It appears he now believes consciousness to be independent of the brain. What will he believe 20 years from now? What do you believe?

As someone who considers herself to be spiritual, I take a very keen interest in neuroscience and have long thought that much of what is taken for spiritual experiences, if not caused by, are definitely related to the brain and nervous system.

Having been born with uncorrected right eye amblyopia (lazy eye) and having struggled academically at school whilst being sensitive and intuitive, it was not until I began having spiritual experiences that I looked for a rational explanation, sure that there was one, since, otherwise, these types of experiences are usually only attributed to mystics or saints.

My investigations into amblyopia and its possible effects on the brain led me to form the hypothesis that the lack of stimulation to the left side of my brain through my lazy right eye caused the right side of my brain, which has historically been associated with spirituality, to work harder. This hypothesis has been borne out by Jill Bolte Taylor's account of her left-brain stroke and her observing hyperactivity in her right brain, which resulted in what we would recognize as metaphysical/mystical experiences.

During my 10-year study of Buddhism, I found the theory came easy; the practice, well, that's another story, I struggled with that, but an intuitive understanding of the Buddhist sutras came easy. Then in 1998, and again in 1999, I experienced the rising of energy called Kundalini.

Thinking about my experiences, there were two possible origins: I could attribute them either to benevolent karma left over from a previous lifetime or to a neuroscientific explanation. I can remember the day I was walking through my local park, asking myself the questions: "Why me" and "Why did these experiences happen to me" and getting a straight three word answer "right brain dominant" and then feeling a little deflated that it wasn't caused by more loftier, more spiritual activity; but, this is what came through and I wasn't going to go against it.

Thus began a period of writing to both psychologists and ophthalmologists to learn more. Most never replied to me; those who did dismissed my hypothesis. I was amazed by their reluctance to accept a rational scientific explanation. Things were said to me like, "If you don't stop looking for a reason, you will lose the gift of the peace and calm that you have been given." In the end, I gave in and shelved my neuroscientific explanation. Even as I was doing so, I felt it was not the right thing to do. I am keenly aware of what goes on in the laboratory of my own body: My thoughts, feelings, and actions are very much guided by this awareness. However, on this occasion, I ignored an inner feeling of uneasiness and started reading all the books I could find on mysticism and spirituality.

In the days following this decision, I noticed that life was not flowing as well as it had been. I felt lost and ungrounded in a way I never had before, attributing my spiritual experiences as being caused by my brain and nervous system. I became ego-inflated, thinking I had been in some way "chosen." The longer it went on, the more superior and ego-inflated I became whilst giving the impression of being the opposite. Then I crashed, or rather my spiritual balloon did, and I came back down to earth with a bang.

I decided to return to my neuroscientific explanation and trust that if this was wrong, it wouldn't be other people who would turn me away from this path again, but the Divine.

Immediately, life began to flow and harmonize once again. I am much stronger now than I had been previously, able to defend the possibility of a link between neuroscience and spirituality. For me, it's now a very simple equation. I have a neuroscientific explanation for my experiences, and life works and flows.

As stated earlier in this book, I believe there is a correlation between spiritual experiences and "something" going on in the brain and nervous system. I am not saying that it is causative because to say it is causative displays a breathtaking arrogance. I am not a neuroscientist, so I cannot speak about cause and effect. However, I do speak of correlation because I often ask myself, "If I had two proper functioning eyes, would I have had the kind of experiences I have had?" Not just the experiences, but their transformative physical, mental, spiritual effects, as well.

Spiritual experiences are common. That they happen is no longer in dispute as they are now so frequently reported. What is less understood is how effective they are in bringing about permanent transformation (i.e., a permanent abiding peace and harmony, not only for those who undergo these experiences, but in the lives of those around them).

A famous spiritual teacher once said that he evaluated the effects of his transmission on his devotees, not only by the changes in their minds and bodies, but also by the changes in their lives and the lives of those around them. Something about this resonated. Authentic spiritual experiences are those that result in such an outflow of peace and compassion that those around them cannot help but be touched. The true purpose of spiritual experience is transformative, both individual and global. And while many people are now reporting energy rising episodes, the world has not yet manifested evidence of transformation. Something is awry.

Why is it that, with so many people reporting spiritual experiences, the world is not transforming? Again, to give a definitive answer would be arrogant. Nevertheless, I suggest it's due in part to the temptation to inflate one's ego that accompanies many spiritual experiences.

I say this based on my own experiences. The spiritual ego distorts the nature and quality of such experiences. It does this by taking ownership and making it "my experience" and then following it with an "I am special" and a "I must teach/ be a guru." I don't believe this is the way of authentic spiritual experience. The Tao behind these experiences is to become even more ordinary (which the ego hates). False spirituality wants us to be Somebody; the real is happy being Nobody. The irony of the process is that you have to desire to become Somebody before you realize that you are Nobody and Nothing. With that realization, you become — not by looking for it — a Somebody who can transform, not only yourself, but more importantly, the world.

WHY BE SPECIAL IF YOU CAN BE YOURSELF?

"What does 'being yourself' mean? It means to be completely natural. To live in the present and to self-express your feelings in each moment."

~ Author

Like a moth drawn irresistibly to the light, I have been drawn every other Sunday to the Satsangs given by the spiritual teacher, Mooji, and broadcast live over the Internet. An inexplicable fascination finds me sitting at my computer, connecting to the broadcast. *Satsang* is the name given to discourses with a spiritual teacher that are meant to accelerate the process of spiritual awakening by burning away everything that we are not, those elements in us that prevent us from emerging.

I have been listening to Mooji for a couple of years now and last year I traveled to London where he was giving these Satsangs because I wanted to ask him a question. Something drew me to him. I only intended to attend one hour of the two-hour Satsang, but even though I put my hand up every time he asked if anyone wanted to speak, he didn't pick me. Because I really wanted to ask my question, I stayed for the next hour. Finally, when I had almost given up hope, he saw my hand up and beckoned for me to come and sit on the stool opposite him.

The first thing he said to me was, "I've seen you; you have been trying for a while!" I was so focused on what I wanted to ask, it didn't register that he had seen me trying to be noticed. I find speaking in public challenging and this time was no exception. I bent down to take the mic that was on the floor and then, not looking at him so that I could formulate my question clearly, I asked, "How do you share spiritual experiences when they are so subjective?" I asked some more about such experiences and when I finally looked up at him, I noticed that he was gazing at me intently.

He said, "First, discover if there is a YOU there to share."

I knew exactly what he meant. He was talking about the difference between the you of the mind and the YOU of no-mind. Words that come from the mind are very different in their tone and impact than words coming from no-mind. Often, words from the mind are bound in ego and motivated by a desire for results. Words from no-mind are motiveless; they come from the depths of nothingness.

Mooji also said to me, "Don't shy away from sharing, but also don't be in too much of a hurry to share." He continued, "Sometimes the mind wants to share and sometimes the deeper power doesn't want to share and then a subtle choice must be made."

I have often thought back to these words, especially when I feel a strong urge to speak, to resist the pull to speak, while examining which part wants to speak and why. And, as the times when I have kept silent while wanting to speak and share have increased, so has the degree of peace and contentment, which I feel also increased. That peace has come from the heart and not the mind, which is why I believe that spiritual awakening is a result of an innocent heart, not a trained mind.

It is so easy to train the mind on the spiritual path. What I saw from watching the last Satsang is that the mind grasps something of the nature of spiritual awakening and plays with it in a different way. Except for one person, everyone who asked Mooji a question was aware that the mind and its thoughts were not who he/she really was. There was an urgency, and in some cases a desperate plea for Mooji to take away their minds. This is nothing more than the mind becoming chameleon-like to avoid being exposed. The innocent heart produces the spontaneous, profound shift of consciousness that characterizes spiritual awakening. Drop the mind and come into the heart.

Jesus said, "Unless you become like little children, you cannot enter the kingdom of heaven." He meant "like little children" in the sense of innocence with a heart filled with wonder, not a child in an immature way, but childlike as opposed to childish. Spiritual awakening is through the heart, not through the mind, no matter how clever the mind thinks it is.

One concern I have with Mooji is that he doesn't give much importance to Kundalini. I feel that he is missing something major in that it is the energy of Kundalini that shifts the consciousness so it awakens. No amount of trying to figure it out with the mind is going to do it. Not accepting the necessary part this energy plays keeps those who sit at Mooji's feet trapped in their minds.

Success in the spiritual journey is reflected in one's level of self-awareness. Okay, suppose this is true: How does one become more self-aware? The first step is to recognize and accept that there is more to our minds than we realize, more, in fact, than we use on a daily basis.

One way of developing self-awareness is to consider pain. When I have a pain, I feel it as separate from myself; therefore, who is it that is feeling the pain? If I was the pain, I wouldn't be able to observe it and see it was separate from me; so, who is it that knows that it's separate? To begin to grasp this is the beginning of self-awareness. Awareness of the Self — which is not the ego self but is another Self, the one that's constantly watching everything that's going on. Not the self that is having a constantly running commentary about what is going on — that is the ego self. So who is it that is watching the constant commentary from a neutral position — just like a mirror reflecting everything without adding or taking away anything? There is something that is watching, not judging. It never judges. It watches dispassionately. Begin to ponder on what it is that is watching and you have made the first breakthrough into self-awareness. Buddhists have termed this watching "witnessing or the witness consciousness."

Don't despair if your efforts to experience this witness consciousness seem futile. In the early days, it's like this. I can remember feeling very frustrated because the moment I came out of mind and connected with the witness, a thought about that connection broke the contact. Keep going and there will come a day when the witness consciousness is permanent and won't require meditation to experience it. Another good practice for cultivating this relationship is mindfulness; in fact, mindfulness is the same as the witness consciousness.

Another effective practice for developing self-awareness is to constantly monitor every thought, feeling, and action. When somebody says or does something to you, notice what effect it has on you. Don't judge the reaction you have as being good or bad, just notice that it is there. On the spiritual journey, the goal is never getting carried away by what someone else says or does, but in recording your reaction to it. The constant question should be: "What is this situation or person showing me about myself?"

Reaction is never about the other, it's always about the ego self. In the past, people used to tell me that I was too hard on myself because I never projected out onto others, I always took it within to see what I could learn from it. Instead of projecting or defending, I used it to develop my own self-awareness.

I took this to the limit. Not only did I identify what it said about me, I judged what I saw as wrong. I judged myself as not kind/generous/patient and then used that to beat myself up and consider myself wrong. This is not the way.

Yes, watch your own reactions, but don't add to them. They're just reactions. You can learn from them, but don't judge them as being right or wrong, or meaning anything about you. Not indicting yourself is the biggest challenge. It leads down a cul-de-sac of needless suffering.

I have learned to examine my reactions to events in my life dispassionately. I am an observer watching everything that happens, but reacting to none of it. And yet...I'm not dead! I have a vibrant love of life and enter fully and completely into what I do. There's nothing vapid or morbid about me. I respond to events rather than react to them and that makes all the difference to my self-awareness and quality of life.

Mooji tells a story of three birds who are on different branches of a tree. The bird on the first branch is busy building a nest, totally engrossed in what it is doing. The bird on the second branch is doing nothing, simply watching the first bird being really busy; and then there is a third bird that is watching both the bird that is doing and the one that is watching. Mooji directs those who are listening to him to the third bird and asks, "What is that bird?" Which suggests to me there is something beyond the second bird — the watcher.

In my spiritual journey, I have experienced the second bird; I leave the significance of the third bird for later.

A couple of years ago, I wanted to ask Mooji a specific question about a woman's ability to become a spiritual master. I believed that a woman could be a devotee, mystic, even spiritually awakened, but a Master...no. That's a job for the boys.

It took me two hours to get to ask my question and when I finally did, I was amazed at Mooji's response. He understood where my question was coming from and spoke about the desire to be a Master. "Why be special, when you can be yourself?" is one of the most profound things he's ever said to me. So, being myself is something to which I am now committed.

What does "being yourself" mean? It means to be completely natural. To live in the present and to self-express your feelings in each moment. This is a challenge for human beings because, for the most part, we hide behind bromides and platitudes. "I'm fine." "Follow your dreams." "Don't mention it." "Have a nice day." "One day at a time."

Being natural and authentic demands that we be honest about our feelings at every moment; because being honest about relations with ourselves and others actually transpire. This is the way of the Tao — effortless action. My spiritual journey has moved from a time when I put so much effort into studying and practicing Mahayana Buddhism to a practice I now qualify as being completely effortless. Every morning, I undertake a spiritual practice, not because of the amount of effort it requires or because I feel I have to do it to sustain a state of peace, calm, or bliss, but because I enjoy it.

The mornings that I don't do it, I acknowledge that I didn't do it and am straight with myself about why — I don't hide behind excuses, reasons, or explanations. To be authentic and natural, it is vital that consciousness is always in the present. Past and future do not exist. The past was once the present and the future will one day be the present so all there is, the present — THE NOW. With naturalness, with nothing forced, a state of enlightenment will reveal itself in the way it is meant to, naturally and effortlessly. Perhaps this is the third bird.

THE I AND ME REVEALED

"Since awakening Kundalini, I am more aware of the idiot or what I call 'me.' This is the part of my being that wants to survive, look good, play it safe; and, then there is the other that I call 'I' that wants to share, contribute, make a difference."
~ Author

During a seminar about living a life that defies the predictable, I learned the story of Colin Wilson, a British philosopher and writer. When he was young, he dreamed about becoming the next Albert Einstein, but at the age of 16 his family fell on hard times and he had to leave school and go to work. He was so unhappy he decided to kill himself.

He took a bottle of hydrochloric acid and was just about to drink it, when he had two insights. The first was that there were two Colin Wilson's within him:

- The first was the idiotic teenager, self-pitying boy who he called his "idiot" and then there was the other Colin Wilson who wanted to make a difference in the world by becoming the next Einstein.
- His second insight was that the "idiot" was going to kill them both.[1]

Since awakening Kundalini, I am more aware of the idiot or what I call "me." This is the part of my being that wants to survive, look good, play it safe; and, then there is the other that I call "I" that wants to share, contribute, make a difference.

At every moment, I get to choose which one I am going to be. Both are there because the "me" was created by the senses (acculturation programming that begins the moment we are born) and is designed for survival, but the "I" was there before the "me." Out of "I" we build "me." When Kundalini rises, it changes the mind and body by working directly on the nervous system to strengthen and balance. But it also expands consciousness so that spiritual writings resonate much more deeply. Kundalini shifts the consciousness from "me" back to "I" where it initially came from. Now I find when I meditate that I watch "me" from the place of "I." This is difficult to explain and I don't want to give the idea of a split personality; this is very much an internal phenomena that doesn't affect interactions with people or with the world.

This realization profoundly affected Eckhart Tolle, who wrote in the *Power of Now* about the moment after he had spent

---

1   Acknowledgement to Landmark Worldwide for this information.

many years suffering from depression when he said to himself, "I cannot live with myself any longer." Suddenly he was struck by the two Eckhart's within him. "I" and "myself" and he asked, "Who is me, and who is myself?" This insight shocked him into realization and has resulted in his becoming a world-famous spiritual teacher. He says after this *he felt himself being drawn up into a vast vortex of energy*, which I assert must have been Kundalini. It was the combination of insight and energy that shifted his consciousness permanently into the state that it is in today.

WHEN KUNDALINI RISES, THERE IS NOWHERE TO HIDE

"Sitting in the seminar filled with shame, and desperately uncomfortable in my chair, I was gripped by this overwhelming urgency to go back to this shop and make amends."
~ Author

While writing this, I posed myself a challenge: Could I write an interesting, but theoretical article or could I write one that, instead of making me look knowledgeable, would reveal how I have been constantly tested since Kundalini rose. Stepping out of my comfort zone, I am going to do the latter. In the past, I have written that awakening Kundalini marks the beginning of authentic spirituality. What do I mean by that? Up to the time Kundalini awakens, one lives in a kind of self-indulgent state that might be summarized as the refusal to be honest with oneself, a very human characteristic. When Kundalini rises, all that stops and the fire of purification begins.

This fire takes many forms. For me, it came in the shape of a seminar I did. I participated in The Money Seminar. One of the weeks (the seminar lasted 10 weeks) was about being authentic and owning up to what we had been less than honest about when it came to money. Smug and complacent in my chair, I sat thinking, "I haven't stolen from anyone and so this conversation doesn't apply to me," when suddenly, from out of nowhere I had a memory of myself as a student working part-time in the corner shop. With a sickening thud in my stomach, I remembered when my friends used to come into the shop. In those days, the till was the type that you keyed the price of things into, so when any of my friends came in, I used to give 5p/10p off whatever they bought. In college, I had a lot of friends! After three months, the owner let me go without giving a reason.

Sitting in the seminar, filled with shame and desperately uncomfortable in my chair, I was gripped by this overwhelming urgency to go back to this shop and make amends. At this point, I was living in a different country and had no idea that the shop would still be there as this had occurred 20 years before! But no matter what my rational mind tried to convince me of (i.e., that it was a fool's mission to go back there), a deeper part of me wasn't listening. I booked a holiday home, factoring in a bus journey that would take me back to the city where the shop was.

I told my mother my plans and she was extremely concerned and responded in the same rationalizing manner my mind had: that this was a crazy thing to do. She did her utmost to talk me out of going. I listened to her concerns patiently and knew at a deep level that my mother wouldn't be the only one that would think this crazy, but there would be few people who understood what was motivating me. I knew what was driving it — Kundalini with its demand for total honesty, integrity, and responsibility.

The day to go back to the shop arrived. I had 300€ in my purse, which is what I reckoned I owed the owner. I boarded the bus, my mind in turmoil but my resolve strong. When we got to the city, I walked through the familiar streets I recognized from my student days. I counted every corner as I turned and with each step, my heart started to beat faster and faster. As I came to the last corner before I could see the shop, I willed that by some miracle it would not be there and I would be spared this ordeal. But that was not to be. When I came around the last corner, there was the exact same shop in all its glory, it didn't even seem to have been redecorated in all that time. Walking slowly towards it, I took a deep breath and opened the door.

The layout was exactly as I remembered it and the man who had given me the job was behind the counter. There were other people in the shop. I walked up to him and said, "Do you remember me?"

He looked at me keenly and said, "Your face seems familiar."

I said, "You employed me years ago when I was a student and I stole from you."

I could see his eyes narrow and I quickly went on, "Not in the way that I put my hands in the till, but when my student friends came in to buy things, I gave them a few pence off everything and I reckon that I owe you 300€, so here it is." And I handed over the 300€ that I had clung onto while walking to the shop.

He took it quickly and put it into his breast pocket then looked at me and said, "Why, after all these years? Why did you come back?"

I said, "It was important for me to come back, take responsibility, and make amends for what I did and this is what I'm doing."

He just looked stunned and said, "Thank you."

I said, "You're welcome," and I turned away and walked out of the shop.

Walking away, I expected to feel high and happy, but I didn't. Exhilarated, but I wasn't. I felt completely drained, exhausted, and incredibly tired. My mind started a rant that could have been my mother's voice about what a stupid thing it was to have done when you don't even feel good after doing it.

I felt so low. I spent the whole bus journey berating myself and analyzing what my expectations were about feeling so flat now. When I got home, my mother was waiting for me and welcomed me with a barrage of questions intermixed with chiding about giving that money to a stranger when there was so much she could have done with 300€.

Totally and utterly spent, I looked at her wearily without the energy to defend myself and said, "I'm going to bed." It was 4:00 PM in the afternoon!

I just couldn't take anymore; I wanted the welcome oblivion of sleep. When I woke up, I felt so different and knew I had made this journey so I could look at myself in the mirror. I ventured out from my bedroom into the kitchen to see my mum with a big smile on her face, saying that while she didn't understand why I had done what I did she was proud of me for having done it.

Before Kundalini rose, my view of my actions would have been "I was only helping my poor student friends; it wasn't really stealing; I didn't gain anything financially by it," but with Kundalini the same actions are viewed very differently and the stark, no-hiding truth emerges, that whatever my reasons, it was stealing and had to be accounted for.

I write this because there is a perception that the rising Kundalini is going to result in a blissful, happy life, some kind of utopia, and while there is much about this energy that does induce those states, there is also the purification aspect, which is real, inexorable, and ongoing. The move of consciousness from the human to the spiritual, which is what the rising of Kundalini accomplishes, is a move to being authentic, living with integrity, and taking responsibility for everything that happens. And this requires courage and humility because nothing can be hidden.

I felt huge internal resistance to doing it, but something drove me and the process really took care of itself! Few are able to expose themselves to being vulnerable. It is only when we are willing to be vulnerable, lose face, and not look good, that something different happens: The ego losing face provides an opening for the Self or Soul to emerge.

CASTING PEARLS BEFORE SWINE

"People are afraid of things that they don't understand and that fear takes many forms — dismissing, rationalizing, faulty logic — strategies the ego uses to prevent the individual who seeks to awaken from recognizing the unreality of who they think they are."
~ Author

Neven Paar's brilliant essay *Spiritual Evolution* hung around in my brain, begging more to be written. In the second paragraph, he writes:

"Don't bother explaining yourself. You will be persecuted if you do. People are afraid of things they don't understand and base their judgments on their fears. Instead, don't speak about the light; BE the light. Become the source of light and lead the way. Others won't understand, but they will be intrigued, inspired. They will follow. Become special through your actions and others will be convinced. You can speak of riches all you want, but once you share them with others, only then will they believe you. Only then will they want to have the riches for themselves, too. This is your purpose. This is why you had an awakening: to open the eyes of others so that they too might see the light as you do. Only then will you be fulfilled. You will find the unity which you seek."[1]

I found myself agreeing wholeheartedly with the first three sentences because it is true that actions, not words, lead the way. Jesus said, "By their fruits, you will know them." He didn't say by their words or what they share. People are afraid of things that they don't understand and that fear takes many forms — dismissing, rationalizing, faulty logic — strategies the ego uses to prevent the individual who seeks to awaken from recognizing the unreality of who they think they are. Just try saying to someone, "You are not who you think you are," and, at least in my case, you will meet with some very funny looks. The safest way to navigate through an awakening — until the awakening experience achieves critical mass — is to BE. Gandhi knew this, "BE the change you want to see in the world." He didn't say speak about, or share this change. He said BE THE CHANGE.

Where I find myself disagreeing with Neven's essay is in the following three sentences: "Become special through your actions and others will be convinced. You can speak of riches all you want but once you share them with others, only then will

1 Spiritual Evolution – Neven Paar, http://www.kundaliniconsortium. org/2013/05/spiritual-evolution.html, 2013.

they believe you. Only then will they want to have the riches for themselves, too."

In my experience, sharing with others doesn't mean others believe me. I am very careful to limit my sharing to what I have experienced, namely the rising of energy up through my spine on two occasions and its corresponding effects.

But the final three sentences from Neven's essay beginning with, "This is your purpose…" stuck with me. There have been times in life when I have read something and it's like the words screamed out at me from the page. Reading these last three sentences was like that. I read them and my soul cried YES. At some level, I know this. At the same time, my ego groaned inwardly as it sensed that, having given up on attempting to touch, move, and inspire people with my experience concerning the transformative energy within all of us, I just might now try again. Reading these last three sentences hit at my very core and woke me up from a tranquilized complacency. A complacency rooted in resignation.

When I found Mahayana Buddhism in 1988, I had no idea that there was anything to be learned from it. I was disillusioned with the Catholic dogma in which I had been brought up. I was unable to validate it through my own experiences, so I began looking for something more authentic. I loved Buddhism for its own sake, not for anything I might "get" from it. When Buddha said it was possible to become awakened in one lifetime — while not initially understanding what he meant — I had a childlike faith in the ultimate truth of his words. Moreover, I didn't want it for myself, but rather for others. This wasn't an ego projection on my part, but a sincere wish to share so that everyone might be able to access the riches within themselves.

As I set off on my Buddhist spiritual journey, wanting only to share my discoveries with others, I found myself feeling unconnected to them, in spite of my passionate desire to become so. The meditation sessions were very difficult. I often felt like quitting, but something kept bringing me back. I was the most reluctant and resistant Buddhist imaginable. Yet, I loved the Buddha passionately. I read all the sutras and complicated Abhidarma texts, but the meditation practice — when I was alone with myself — was torture most of the time.

My discomfort with fellow spiritual people stems from feeling uncomfortable with anything that smacks of specialness. Looking back now, I realize I sensed the presence of spiritual egotism without knowing its provenance. I sensed the veiled superiority that many on a spiritual path exude. I wanted to distance myself from it; yet, I craved the teachings. It was the teachings and an overwhelming inner pull that kept me in the Buddhist environment for almost 10 years.

Then, in 1998, I experienced the first rising of energy up my spine, in a non-Buddhist, non-spiritual setting. Being familiar with mindfulness through meditation, I connected fully to the energy and noticed that it didn't appear to move too far up my spine, but the effects of this experience in the weeks and months following were transformative — physically, mentally, and emotionally.

There were so many theories flying around about this energy that it was easy to become lost. I heard so many accounts of energy — often referred to as Kundalini — rising up the spine. And, with each account, I found myself referring back to my own experience, as it was the only authentic evidence I had. I could not rely on interpretations of the experience, only on the actual experience, the actual rising of the energy and its corresponding effects.

Because this experience was not accompanied by any great spiritual insights and because I had no idea that this energy existed, I didn't speak about it much. I didn't share with people because I didn't think that it meant anything.

So, where is this going? Back to Neven's words, "Only when you share them with others, will they then believe you." This has not been my experience. I began to speak and share. I was met with either blank looks or avoidance of eye contact. Rapid excuses to leave, to go or do something else. For about a year, I shared openly in a blog that I wrote reverently about the physical, mental, and spiritual changes I was undergoing using my body as a laboratory. I wrote and shared until, eventually, I was written and shared out. To have a relatively smooth spiritual awakening, there must be a desire to share the fruits with others. It comes down to a question and an attitude. The question, "Why do I want this?". The attitude, "I don't want it just for me." These are critical because ultimately we are all one and so not wanting awakening/enlightenment for oneself alone validates the faith that we are all one.

After my second experience with this energy a year later in a spiritual setting when the energy went to my brain and descended to my heart, I experienced deep love and compassion for everything. Now that my ego has been largely subdued (not totally, because it never can be), the drive I had to share, speak, and to be seen as special has disappeared. In the early weeks and months of awakening, the wish to be recognized as special is there as the ego prepares to defend itself because it recognizes that the awakening experience poses a threat to its survival.

Before reading Neven's essay, I was the prisoner in Plato's cave allegory who escapes and realizes the unreality in which his fellow prisoners are living. He races back to share with them what he has realized and they kill him because they don't understand and don't want to be jolted out of their accepted perceptions. The world we live in is much like that. Those of us who are awakened see the unreal world of the unawakened not as inferior, but as unnecessarily limiting. Thanks to Neven's essay, I realized I had sold out on what might be possible if I don't hide out.

And yet, just talking and sharing is not enough. The only thing that awakens is experience and until those of us who are awakened can provide this for others, all we do is cast pearls before swine. I sometimes watch a YouTube *satsang* that Mooji gives. I marvel at the frustration of people in the video who sit at his feet. Intuitively, they know he is living another reality, but they are unable to access it for themselves. With a mixture of story, parable, and direct confrontation with their egos, Mooji tries to transfer his vision, but without the ability to confer what is known in the East as Shaktipat — direct guru transmission of energy to enable the consciousness to awaken and shift from its identification with the body/mind — he seems unable to make much progress as the same people come to sit at his feet time and time again. This leaves me with the question: Is it worthwhile speaking or sharing when it isn't accompanied by the grace of awakening?

KUNDALINI IS A GIFT

"Manic-like symptoms seem to be an inevitable part of a Kundalini awakening. The energy activates dormant areas in the brain, giving rise to an influx of new ideas and connections with little ability to be objective or witness these thoughts. At this stage, there is little to be gained by trying to bring the consciousness down from its lofty heights because the person cannot hear it."

~ Author

This week a man I'll call John phoned me to say that he'd had a Kundalini experience three years ago and his life was "falling apart." I immediately recognized this "falling apart" syndrome as the mind creating fear through its incessant chatter.

If I opened up the brain and body of this man, I wouldn't find any "falling apart." I would find certain sensations, bodily experiences, thoughts, attitudes, but no "falling apart." I tried to slow his mind down by asking him to be specific about what he meant by "falling apart."

"What are the thoughts, feelings, perceptions, attitudes you are having? The actions you are having trouble with?"

The difficulty he had in isolating what he meant showed me the degree to which the conceptual mind was running the show, and how much his mental activity was based on fear.

Interestingly, or one could say ironically, he only used spiritual practices to ease the chronic back pain he had, saying that in the course of a five-minute spiritual exercise, energy coursed up through his body and "everything changed."

I was reminded of my state of mind three years into the experience: manic, making all kinds of connections, seeing synchronicities everywhere. Listening to him, I was fascinated; it was like listening to an earlier version of myself.

Manic-like symptoms seem to be an inevitable part of a Kundalini awakening. The energy activates dormant areas in the brain, giving rise to an influx of new ideas and connections with little ability to be objective or witness these thoughts. At this stage there is little to be gained by trying to bring the consciousness down from its lofty heights because the person cannot hear it. At least, I couldn't. I was too busy ringing up Kundalini yoga teachers berating them for advocating the raising of this energy without any information about the karmic history of the individuals in their classes.

At that time, I had little trust in Kundalini, even though my own experience had been smooth. Yet, I sensed its power intuitively.

Looking back now at those conversations, I must have sounded so weird to the teachers who answered the phone and listened to my rant! If someone had tried to speak to me about "calming down" and "witnessing," I would have probably felt angry and unlistened to.

I realized it was the same situation with John. So, I gave up any idea of talking with him about watching his thoughts without identifying or becoming absorbed with them, and I decided to meet him on his own terms. Doing so involved speaking about the manic ideas of religious conspiracies I'd had at the same stage of the process. I advised him not to do any spiritual practices and to find something that he could give his Word to (what I mean by Word is to do what you said you would do when the mind says "it's the worst thing you could do"). Something that diverted his fascination with the contents of his consciousness, which are merely the result of an awakened Kundalini working on the nervous system.

The best way to do this is to make Word more important than WANT. In saying this to him, a part of me hoped he would listen and find something he could commit to that would divert his attention from the spiritual pitfalls of self-absorption and fascination. But at this stage, advice like this is not really heard. The ego mind is too busy trying to reassert the control that was lost when Kundalini rose for the first time. It recognizes that the same ego-state is not possible because consciousness has shifted, but there still exists a small window of possibility for a spiritual ego, which is where the insights, connections, and synchronicities come from. I'm not for one moment saying that these are not real: Witnessing and acknowledging that they are happening is perfectly okay. However, becoming absorbed and fascinated by them constitutes a stumbling block in the process. I have not experienced the entire range of physical, mental, and spiritual transformation which Kundalini induces. Yet, I see its effects very much on the brain and nervous system. Beyond that, I can't comment.

In 2013, I organized the First UK Conference on Kundalini. I had high hopes that the conference would promote greater understanding of Kundalini. Now I realize that Kundalini is different for everyone. There are no pat answers or sure ways of either raising or living with it. It is very much a path by the Alone for the Alone. Yes, there are fellow travelers who share their journeys, but their journeys are not yours — you have to go through them alone. Just remember it is not Kundalini that is going to throw you off the path, leaving you in a spiritual wasteland, but your own mind with the thoughts it conjures up.

I wrote about the Internet Satsangs, given by Mooji and the people sitting at his feet, either laughing hysterically (having apparently got the cosmic joke!) or else "falling apart," as John put it. One lady explained that she was "falling so apart," she went to the doctor who gave her antidepressants that she takes, but doesn't want to. Mooji asked her one question, "Do you take these tablets when you are sleeping?" Confused, the woman replied, "No."

Listening to this, something hit me and I asked myself: What happens during sleep that does not happen during the day? The answer came to me so clearly: mind. At night, the mind is asleep and there are therefore no thoughts of "falling apart," so the unbearable fear that accompanies such a thought cannot and does not occur. In that moment, I was grateful to Mooji for the insight I'd had. Kundalini is a gift. It is the mind about which you have to be vigilant.

BEING HUMAN IS ONLY A GAME

"I was trying to rid myself of ego! By blaming myself for everything, putting myself down at every opportunity, and being annoyingly humble, I thought I could purify myself."
~ Author

L ying in bed one morning this week just before fully waking up, in that state of no-thought for a few seconds, I realized that life is nothing but a game. Letting this realization permeate, I had the insight that in the beginning there was NOTHING but the I AM, pure undifferentiated space. After a time, the I AM got bored with being all there was and decided to create a game by dividing itself in two, the I AM and I AM NOT. So, like a cloud that splits itself in two, the I AM split into two and became a game where one part played the other (i.e., I AM vs. AM NOT).

Many years ago, I read *Conversations with God-Book One* by Neale Donald Walsch. Since then, I have reread it at least seven times because its ideas resonate so deeply. I realize I have been pondering the ideas contained in this book for many years, which is why my experiences jibe so completely with a book the author claims is a direct communication with the Divine through automated writing.

On page 22 he says, "In the beginning, that which Is is all there was, and there was nothing else. Yet All That Is could not know itself — because All That Is is all there was, and there was nothing else. And so, All That Is...was not. For in the absence of something else, All That Is, is not."

But this was no fun because I AM or, the All That Is, knew it still was. It knew that it was also I AM NOT, so it had to make the game more exciting and the I AM chose to forget it had created the I AM NOT and the whole game of being human began: seeing through the illusion of the I AM NOT to reveal the I AM, out of which paradoxically the I AM NOT came anyway.

This is why sages have said that we end up where we start because there is nothing but awareness, or I AM. We are all the I AM and we have created others and the world as the I AM NOT, but that is an illusion, a game every human being plays. In spiritual awakening, the game is seen for what it is, a sardonic cosmic joke played on human beings.

And yet the game remains hidden. As Kundalini gradually rises, the game is revealed as a game, at least that is how it happened for me. Before Kundalini rose, I had read about the *Divine Leela* or the Divine Play, but I didn't understand or realize its significance. The realization came out of the rising energy. Others have realized "the cosmic game" without attributing it to Kundalini, which makes me think that the ultimate realization is not dependent on Kundalini rising and it is I that made the link causal (i.e., the ultimate realization being the result of Kundalini).

So what if it's not. What if it's the result of learning to be self-observant — being careful to be honest and authentic about what resonates for me as truth and what I can validate by my experience?

I remember a spiritual teacher once saying, "So if you want Enlightenment, then you must be prepared to get into a street fight with yourself'." You have to stop projecting blame on others and turn the light inwards — be honest about what is going on inside of you. Getting into a street fight with yourself or the I AM NOT means the end of blame and the beginning of responsibility.

It's not easy, for taking responsibility doesn't mean turning the blame on yourself, either. This is a mistake I made for many years, blaming myself for everything.

People have said I was too hard on myself, and looking back I can see that I was. I was trying to rid myself of ego! By blaming myself for everything, putting myself down at every opportunity, and being annoyingly humble, I thought I could purify myself. Lurking beneath this false humility was a quietly growing spiritual ego that looked down on those not following a declared spiritual path. Thinking back on my folly, I cringe as I write this. But as others have noted: authenticity and honesty, as well as vigilance and awareness, are required on this path. Now I am much kinder to myself and life is magical and wonderful in so many different ways.

THE DIVIDED BRAIN AND THE MAKING OF THE WESTERN WORLD

"As I re-listened to Jill Bolte's TED talk, *Stroke of Insight*, I was once again struck by her conviction that it's a matter of choice whether we operate from the left or the right in life."
~ Author

A while ago, I collected Iain McGilchrist's book, *The Master and His Emissary* — the one that inspired the subtitle for this chapter — from the post office and once outside tore off the distinctly Amazon brown cardboard, releasing the book from bondage. The first thing that struck me was how thick it was (over 500 pages). I didn't realize there was so much to say about the right brain, or more specifically, about the divided brain.

I waited for a bus to take me to work and, once on, flipped through the first few pages. As I read, I felt this over-whelming relief, a sense of coming home to everything I had been thinking. I was filled with such gratitude for the universal guidance, which has never let me waver from my faith that I am right-brain dominant. What Iain does in this book is get away from the stark dichotomy of right and left, thereby alleviating the associated criticisms and dismissals that have been the fate of similar works in the past.

In the past, when compared to the right hemisphere of the brain, the left has always come out of these studies lacking — namely, being seen as reasonable and boring as opposed to exciting and creative. Iain stresses that this research is more complicated and that most capabilities involve both sides of the brain. Yet, from what he has written, there is no doubt that he believes the right governs different aptitudes than the left.

This is exciting because if consciousness is shifting from the left to the right, then knowing how the right brain operates is going to make the shift less stressful and provide a context for it to happen. It may also explain the frequency of people reporting spiritual awakening-type experiences.

I scanned the book to see if there was any mention connecting the brain with vision that might provide an explanation for why I am right-brain dominant (my hypothesis being that an uncorrected, lazy right eye has not adequately stimulated my left brain so my right has had to compensate by being more active). On page 26 Iain states, "If you are a bird, you solve the conundrum of how to eat and stay alive by employing different strategies with either eye: the right eye (left hemisphere) for getting and feeding, the left eye (right hemisphere) for vigilant awareness of the environment." I'm not a bird, but it left me wondering what happens if there is a lack of visual stimulation from the right eye to the left hemisphere? Does the right brain work harder to compensate, in the same way one kidney does double duty when the other one stops working? It seems logical that it would.

I checked the index to see if there was any mention of spirituality or Kundalini. There wasn't, but I wasn't surprised, as spirituality has not been identified as a right brain activity, much less Kundalini as a manifestation of it. Nevertheless, when I am on this track, inspirational notions come to me. For instance, this morning, on waking, I remembered a TED talk by neuroscientist, Dr. Jill Bolte Taylor in which she watched herself having a stroke and experienced her consciousness leave her left brain and enter the right brain. This raises another question (i.e., is it the brain itself or is it the movement of consciousness?). Is either side of the brain inert until fired up by consciousness?

As I re-listened to Jill Bolte's TED talk, *Stroke of Insight*, I was once again struck by her conviction that it's a matter of choice whether we operate from the left or right in life.

What does this mean? That no matter what people say, if something doesn't feel right, then it's not. So, rather than giving in, stay steady, ask for universal guidance to provide the answer, and keep vigilant and alert.

In the face of criticism, it's all too easy to give up on our deepest truth. This is the challenge of being human...to stay true to what we believe and what feels authentic. Over the years, many people have tried to tell me that my profound spiritual experiences and their accompanying states of consciousness are the result of karma or spiritual effort; but, I have always known deep down that there is something else in play, and I have stayed steady in the conviction that the something else is related to my right-brain dominance. The details of this hypothesis are not yet fully cognizable, but they are coming together.

In the West, left-brain dominance, knowledge, and knowing have been all important, even in spiritual pursuits.[1] Those who could remember and recite spiritual literature were seen as gurus, and they were followed in the belief that the states of spiritual consciousness alluded to in spiritual literature could be transmitted. Many devotees were disappointed when they found out this state couldn't be transmitted, or at least not transmitted in a permanent and lasting way. *That which Knows cannot Experience.* These are two different worlds. To go from one to the other requires a shift.

On page 79, McGilchrist makes a fascinating (at least for me) distinction between left and right in terms of certainty:

"The left hemisphere likes things that are man-made. Things we make are also more certain: We know them inside out, because we put them together. They are not, like living things, constantly changing and moving, beyond our grasp. Because the right hemisphere sees things as they are, they are constantly new for it, so it has nothing like the databank of information about categories that the left hemisphere has."

This got me thinking about the ego and how it's an entity that human beings construct from the way we interpret ourselves, and from the sensory information we ingest from the world around us. It is formalized as we acquire language and then for the rest of our lives, we fight tooth and nail to maintain these constructs, which take the form of being right and defending a point of view.

This is not wrong. If taken from the perspective of what is written about the left brain in McGilchrist's book, it is a simply a structure we have put together. If we are aware of the tendency of the left brain to be rigid and inflexible, then we can choose to shift — as choice is always possible with awareness. In ignorance, choice is not possible.

On page 80, McGilchrist goes on to say, "The right hemisphere is virtually silent, relatively shifting and uncertain,

---

1   *The Master and his Emissary,* Iain McGilchrist, Yale University Press, 2012, pp. 78

where the left hemisphere by contrast may be unreasonably, even stubbornly, convinced of its own correctness."

This makes sense to me because of how reluctant people are to shift their points of view or validate their opinions. There is a rigid correctness in the left brain, which doesn't allow for the right brain to express itself, which, in turn, really doesn't care about being right (no pun intended!).

To say that I am heavily involved with this book at the moment is an understatement. I am poring over each word in each sentence and resonating with all of it. For the first time in many years, I feel the excitement that comes from experiencing authenticity, having finally found something that mirrors my thoughts and feelings about this topic.

This is an important book. If there wasn't the shift happening from the left brain to the right, I wouldn't be so excited, but it is happening. You only have to Google "spiritual awakenings" and you will find YouTube videos created by people speaking about this shift, which doesn't usually happen in the same way for any two people, but whose effects and realizations are experienced in similar ways. Depending on the quality of consciousness and the degree of awareness, the means are different.

I don't want anything I write or quote about this book to be seen as a value judgment on the qualities of either hemisphere of the brain. Of course, I am biased towards the right brain because I filter my experiences through it. Nevertheless, the left is needed to organize what is experienced and give voice to the experiences of the right brain. The left has asserted mastery over the right for too long and must now assume the role of interpreter for right-brain perception and experience.

When I was training to teach Kundalini yoga, one of the qualification requirements was to do a *kriya* (a set of postures designed to have a specific effect on the body) for 40 consecutive days. Because Kundalini works on the nervous system, the number of consecutive days that one practices a certain kriya or meditation has a definite effect. According to Yogi Bhajan, who brought Kundalini yoga from the East to the West, there is a natural 40-day rhythm to the habits of the body and mind. It takes 40 days of consistent practice to break a habit or for Kundalini to act on the nervous system. It takes 90 days of consistent practice to establish new neural pathways (a new habit) and 120 days to establish that habit permanently.

The 40 days have to be consecutive, so if I missed one, I had to begin all over again. Since I wasn't sure about my ability to sustain this, I decided to start the day after my first weekend of teacher training in December 2010. The purpose of the kriya we selected was to strengthen and balance the third chakra. It involved a number of abdominal exercises, which have never been my favorites. The third chakra is all about power and will.

The 40 days were to run over Christmas of 2010. The day after Christmas 2010, my dad died. In the days following his death, I continued my kriya. On the evening we brought him home from the hospital to spend the night before being buried the next morning — a custom in Irish funerals — I went to bed at 12:00 AM — got up at 3:00 AM, had a cold shower, did my kriya, and then sat with my dad, playing the music he loved until my mum got up at 8:00 in the morning and we buried him.

I finished the 40 days, so euphoric at the end. It wasn't easy, especially the final five days. I had battled with my mind, which had had enough of it. Yet, the thought of beginning again — if I missed one day — acted as such a spur, that on the last day, even though it was late in the evening when I completed it...I completed it. It was done.

Looking back, I can see how the right and left brains played their respective roles. In the early days of doing the kriya, it was a fresh and new, pure experience, the domain of the right brain. Then, as the days wore on, I observed how the left brain began to categorize the timing of certain exercises so I could recognize when a certain point in the music arrived, indicating there was only one minute before the timer was due to go off, signifying the end of a particular exercise. I could also see how, as the exercises in the kriya became more familiar and automatic, more thoughts would surface — mostly on how bored I was. It was as if the left brain used the vacuum created by the novelty of becoming familiar with the kriya to bombard me with thoughts.

When something is new, fresh, unfamiliar, the right brain uses spacial and muscle memory to grasp the whole, and then, as the operation becomes familiar, the elements of that experience are "processed and managed" by the left brain — categorized and made familiar, which, counterproductively, it would seem, renders the experience lifeless and inert. For me, when this happened the kriya became something I did rather than experienced.

Perhaps it's inevitable that the left brain does this with any new experience; perhaps it's a way of making space for the right brain to take on new experiences. From my perspective as a right-brain dominant individual, it is only since Kundalini rose that I have been able to find the words to describe my experiences. Kundalini has activated more of my left brain so I can now classify and make sense of my experiences and for this reason I have come to realize its value in expanding consciousness. Without the input of the left brain, there would be no art or poetry, only experience without expression, which is fine if you want to be a mystic, but not so fine if there is any inclination to inspire people about what's possible.

THE POWER OF COMPASSION

"There is a disconnect between knowing we should be more compassionate and not being so, which begs the question: Why? What is it that stops us from being more compassionate?"
~ Author

Many years ago, I volunteered to work with Crisis over the Christmas period. Crisis is a charity in England that provides shelters for homeless men and women over the festive period. I completed the application form and filled in the shift booking form.

Two weeks before Christmas, I received a letter saying that I had been accepted. It included instructions and directions on where to go and what to do on the first morning of my shift. I don't remember what my motivation was for working with Crisis as I had never done it before. Maybe I had heard someone speak about it and how great it was and thought, "Sounds good, I'll give it a go." I felt quite excited after getting the confirmation letter.

I arrived early on the morning of my shift and was there with about 10 other volunteers. During the roll call of volunteers, I noted that some had not shown up. We were then assigned to Crisis employees for training. I was assigned to the Alcoholics Shelter! I really didn't know what to make of it or what it might mean for me.

The shelter was in North London and I noticed the great atmosphere the minute I entered. Music was playing. There was a dayroom, a canteen, and sleeping quarters. On each shift, I was in charge of something different. One shift, it might be giving out food in the canteen; on another shift, handing out donated clothes and shoes as presents. Some nights, I passed the time speaking with different men and women. After hearing so many heartbreaking stories on these shifts, I realized how easy it is to become homeless. All it takes is a few incidents that result in life spiraling out of control and people losing everything. It opened my eyes.

There was a notice board in the dayroom. One day, I was looking at it and saw a poem that a man named Jamie had written — about life on the streets. The rawness and purity of it spoke to me, so I went to find him. Asking around, one of the women pointed to a man in his late 30s, early 40s. I went up to him and told him how much I loved his poetry. He smiled and simply said, "I only learned to read and write six months ago." I was stunned, and yet deep down I recognized that his creativity was coming from somewhere fresh and different.

I asked him if he would tell me his story. Here is what he said:

"On the streets for years, an alcoholic and a drug addict, I was walking across Westminster Bridge one evening when I met a girl who was desperate for drugs. I felt so sorry for her that I gave her the drugs I had for myself. I bought some more; but, for some reason I couldn't take them so I threw them in the river. A few evenings later, I'm sitting in a shop doorway when this man tries to give me a leaflet. I said to him, 'It's no good giving that to me, mate. I can't read or write.' He asked me if I wanted to learn and I said, 'Sure.' And for three months, he came every week to teach me to read and write. At the end, he asked me to join some religious group that he was part of, but I said, 'No.' Now I spend my time reading and writing poetry."

I left Jamie, touched and moved by his story, and also having no doubt about the power of compassion. My regret is that I never asked him for one of his poems. The last I heard about him was that he was reading English at Cambridge University. I believe that the compassion he showed to a stranger turned his life around in such a dramatic way.

The value of compassion is widely recognized, and there is even a specific therapy called compassion focused therapy. There is also a Charter for Compassion, which has over 100,000 signatures; but, if you look at the world, it doesn't seem as though it's becoming more compassionate.

There is a disconnect between knowing we should be more compassionate and not being so, which begs the question: Why? What is it that stops us from being more compassionate? One reason might be because we are too self-absorbed, so much so that we just don't see the other, never mind act with compassion. But rather than labeling our entire species as selfish, could it be that we are naturally compassionate, but showing compassion is painful, especially when we can't do anything about it? So, we close this aspect of ourselves down. This is why many spiritual awakening experiences result in compassion — the flowering of that which is already within.

KUNDALINI AND FEAR

"Gradually, if the mind is not listened to, the expansion of consciousness that an awakening experience produces becomes integrated, resulting in peace, joy, harmony, clarity — a life that flows and has balance."
~ Author

Many years ago I came across an old Sufi story that resonated with me. I don't know why. The story goes that there is a big black dog who is extremely thirsty. Every time it goes to the well to take a drink, it looks in and sees another big dog looking out, so it becomes afraid and moves away. Eventually, the thirst gets too to be much and the dog just jumps in the well and, of course, the other dog disappears.

I understand that the big dog looking out from the well is the mind. The mind throws up all kinds of fearful thoughts when it feels its authority is being threatened. In the writings of realized mystics and sages, fear at one point or another has to be dealt with. Not a crippling or paralyzing fear, but a fear that must be experienced and overcome in order for one to awaken spiritually.

In my own case, when Kundalini rose the second time, I was on a meditation retreat and experienced the rising and falling of this energy. I had heard about the concept of surrender during the 10 years I spent studying and practicing Mahayana Buddhism and had considered it to be the end of the spiritual journey. During one of the occasions of the rising energy I murmured "I surrender" and thought that would be the end of it. But it wasn't, and in that moment when I realized I had come to the end of everything I had known, I felt a twinge of fear. It didn't last very long, but it was there. Being brought to this place of fear and then having the courage to go beyond it is a characteristic of spiritual awakening.

I know my mind created this fear by the thought, "I don't know what else to do." Then, following the experience, the mind quickly let loose a stream of other thoughts like "What happened," "You're going mad." Following a spiritual awakening, the mind tends to do this because it feels threatened by the sudden expansion of consciousness. These thoughts only last a short while. That's why staying steady and not acting on the streaming chatter coming from the mind is important. Observing how the mind behaves, without getting absorbed or drawn in, is the key.

I can remember in the months following the Kundalini rising having the words of the hymn I learned when I was in a Catholic boarding school in my head constantly: "Do not be afraid." I would say them repeatedly to myself to manage the fear, which at times became quite acute, as the mind tried its hardest to throw me off course.

Gradually, if the mind is not listened to, the expansion of consciousness that an awakening experience produces becomes integrated, resulting in peace, joy, harmony, clarity — a life that flows and has balance. But this is not possible without confronting fear and when that fear is faced, it turns out not to be fear at all, but only a projection of a threatened mind.

KUNDALINI: HOW AND WHY IT CAN GO WRONG

"'Know thyself' is essential for a successful Kundalini rising that leads to a spiritual awakening and not to a fragmentation of consciousness from which it is difficult to return to normal everyday life and consciousness. It is unfortunate that so many on the spiritual path do not want to take the time to complete this necessary stage."
~ Author

Kundalini is our basic evolutionary energy that lies dormant at the base of the spine in the first chakra called *Mooladhara*, or the root chakra. When consciousness attains a certain stage of development, Kundalini rises to accelerate the process. It marks the shift from the fourth human kingdom to the fifth spiritual kingdom. First, there is mineral, then plant, then animal, finally human; and then we move into the spiritual through the vehicle of Kundalini.

When Kundalini is activated by exceptional means(i.e. by trauma or shock), it tries to move up to meet Shiva in the seventh chakra at the crown of the head. Normally, it should progress through the central *Sushumna* nerve in the etheric energy web of the spine. When it encounters blocked energy in the first three chakras, it moves up through the side nerves, either *Pingala* or *Ida*. When it moves up through the *Pingala* nerve, the subject feels heat; and, when it moves up through the *Ida* nerve, the subject feels cold.

Neither of these is the correct way and neither reaches the crown of the head to enable the seventh chakra to open to receive the descending Kundalini. Descending and ascending together completes the energy circuit the awakened Kundalini uses to travel around the body via the nervous system, which must remain unobstructed for Kundalini to manage its work.

That is why I put so much emphasis on self-development and self-awareness work because it is necessary before thinking about raising Kundalini. "Know thyself" is essential for a successful Kundalini rising that leads to a spiritual awakening and not to a fragmentation of consciousness from which it is difficult to return to normal everyday life and consciousness. It is unfortunate that so many on the spiritual path do not want to take the time to complete this necessary stage. I admit it is difficult. Stirring up repressed psychological elements is not pleasant, but refusing to confront them keeps energies blocked in the chakras with no hope of real spiritual awakening.

In my own case, I did this self-development work after Kundalini rose. I had studied and practiced Tibetan Mahayana

Buddhism for almost 10 years before it rose, so I had uncon-sciously prepared myself to withstand the force of Kundalini. When it rose, I was ready...to a point, but there is no escaping the necessity of doing self-awareness work.

Kundalini is only concerned with truth and authenticity. When we have the courage to face the truth about ourselves and our lives, the Truth sets us free. Kundalini can then work the way it was designed to. Without self-awareness work, Kundalini continues to affect the nervous system in various ways without reaching its ultimate goal of spiritual awakening and self-real-ization.

AVOID THE SPIRITUAL PATH IF YOU ARE AFRAID

"This altered consciousness is so profound and, at the same time, so deeply threatening to the mind that, in the days and weeks following my experience, the mind threw up all kinds of fearful thoughts as to what the experience meant and the possible consequences of being called to a celibate life as a nun, which I had no interest in."

~ Author

The first question a reader might ask is 'why' — what is there on the spiritual path to be afraid of? I have often thought that any spiritual book or practice should come with a health warning that says, "From the moment you open this book and/or take on this practice, your life is not going to be the same." The minute one says "yes" to the spiritual, no matter how tentative that yes may be, new neural patterns are laid down in the brain that one day, if the conditions are right, could result in a Kundalini awakening.

My spiritual journey began when I was nine and has continued on and off up to the present. The most intense period were the years I spent studying and practicing Tibetan Mahayana Buddhism. Pulled along by some invisible force I didn't understand, not knowing why I was doing it, I knew that something bigger was propelling me along this path. I would sit in meditation and be totally and completely bored, vowing, "This is the last time I am going to put myself through this." Once the session was over, my memory seemed to be wiped clean of the torture I had suffered so that when it came time for the next sitting, I walked meekly in like a lamb going to slaughter — the slaughter of being alone with the contents of my own mind — and no escape.

I thought life would get easier, be smooth and harmonious. In fact, the opposite happened. My relationships with people seemed to be even more fraught, and my despair at ever being understood only escalated. At one point, I asked myself, "Why do I continue to meditate and pursue a spiritual path when life just seems to get more and more difficult?" Still I persisted.

What have I retained from so many years of dedication? A practice like meditation brings deeply buried issues to the surface. I endured years of uncertainty.

For a long time it seems no water is going into the bucket — the practice merely releases pain, and then one day there's an experience — and the bucket is overflowing. It's important to keep a practice going, no matter what is happening in everyday life. It's easy to give up when the results aren't noticeable, but the spiritual path is like water dripping into a bucket; it's not an overnight thing.

Courage is essential on the spiritual path. In the face of fear and uncertainty, the path is as narrow as a razor's edge. There are many places where consciousness can get stuck. There is no guidebook for the expansion of consciousness, specifically for YOU. Or, perhaps, there are too many. The writings of the sages and saints, yes, but the journey by the Alone to the ALONE is done alone and requires courage.

The first spiritual experience is of greatest importance. In my case, the overflowing water resulted in a first rising of energy from the base of my spine (Kundalini). This experience shifted my consciousness from without to within. Instead of looking outward, I focused completely on the energy within. This altered perspective that consciousness takes on, changes knowledge into experience, which ultimately becomes wisdom.

After it happened, spiritual literature became a source of validation for my experience rather than a source of seemingly unattainable knowledge. This altered consciousness is so profound and, at the same time, so deeply threatening to the mind, that in the days and weeks following my experience, the mind threw up all kinds of fearful thoughts as to what the experience meant and the possible consequences of being called to a celibate life as a nun, which I had no interest in. Staying steady in the face of these kind of thoughts takes courage, and I am forever grateful to my years of Buddhist training for keeping me steady during what were often scary and uncertain moments.

If you are not prepared and willing to live life from a place of uncertainty, then do not go near the spiritual path. It is not what you think it is. In 1988, I had no idea when I went to my first Buddhist class that there was a powerful, spiritually-transformative energy lying dormant within the body that would make itself known to me and shift me physically, mentally, and spiritually. I was drawn to it. I loved the Buddha without any expectation of material or other sort of benefit. And while life is truly balanced and harmonious now, it wasn't always so.

There are so many surprises on the spiritual path, unexpected rewards that are incompatible with fear, which is why I say, "Do not approach the spiritual path if you are afraid. Stay with the known. Don't venture into the choppy waters of the unknown."

SPIRIT WANTS ONLY TO FLY

"It is our subtle body and not the gross physical body that responds to Spirit. The response is different for different vehicles depending on the filter through which they interpret them."
~ Author

The poet Rainer Maria Rilke is the inspiration for the title of this chapter because it helped me answer a question that I have pondered since the death of Nelson Mandela: Why do great leaders of Mandela's caliber die? It seems like we continuously reinvent the leadership and spiritual wheel, particularly the latter. Reading about the lives of the great saints and mystics, and the tribulations they overcame to achieve realization — only to die — emphasizes the vacuum that devotees of these great masters do their best to fill. Their followers are never equal to the task because the mind and heart of the founder is no longer present. So, when I came across this poem, it answered a lot for me.

The Spirit Flies Free
If I don't manage to fly, someone else will.
The spirit wants that there be flying.
And for who happens to do it,
In that he has only a passing interest.

After reading and pondering it for a while. I realized that the physical vehicle isn't important. It is merely the substantiated form through which Spirit flies. The challenge for Spirit is to find willing vehicles through which to fly. Ultimately, all vehicles die. What is important and permanent is the flying. And yet Spirit doesn't fly exactly the same way through every vehicle, as the lives and writings of the great realizers vary one from the other. Why is this? If it's one Spirit, why are its manifestations different?

The differences that emerge are the result of the mind interpreting the energetic effects of Spirit. It is our subtle body and not the gross physical body that responds to Spirit. The response is different for different vehicles, depending on the filter through which they interpret them. In my own case, my experience of Spirit, which I see as Kundalini, was very much an energy that rose from the base of my spine up through my body — a kind of Spirit ascension. For some, it's an experience of energy descending from above. In either case, the same energy, but the reports of the observer (from memory) and the level of consciousness attained determines how it will be interpreted and, more importantly, what it means. For human beings, everything means something; the impulse to seek meaning is hardwired into us so that the brain can make sense of the world.

Many Masters have warned against the lure of Spirit and its manifestations (i.e., visions, lights, etc.), and have pointed out that spiritual experiences are not realizations and to seek the former at the expense of the latter is going down a blind alley. When devotees spoke to Osho about such experiences, he downplayed them, pointing out that it made very little difference to the devotee's ultimate state of realization, suggesting that these experiences be let go, just as one drops a bag of rubbish into a bin. He was always at pains to point out that spiritual experiences are not IT.

The more profound the experience, the more difficult it is to let it go. So, when I was first told to let my experience go — to not allow myself to become absorbed by it or to let it disturb my everyday, normal life — I was reluctant to do so. I felt that something special had happened, and I didn't want to forget about it or let it go. It is only now, so many years later, that I understand why it is essential to let this kind of experience go. It is because everything changes, even the nature of spiritual experience; and, to hold onto it is to limit what is possible in the future. It is necessary to let go of the known to make space for the unknown, moving from the known to the unknown to that which is unknowable, thus fulfilling our purpose as spiritual human beings.

BOLDNESS – BORN OF COMPASSION

"Today, intense meditation like Goenka can be done relatively safely with the knowledge that the effects of energy work bear much quicker results now than before. This puts the responsibility for informing students about the dormant energy and its effects on the teachers of spiritual practices to make sure that students are aware of the power and risks before undertaking a given practice.

~ Author

In the early hours of one morning this week, I received a text from a woman distressed about the effects of rising energy that occurred while she was on a Buddhist meditation retreat. She asked if I could help her. As it was too early for me to do anything constructive, I drifted back to sleep.

On waking again, my first thought was of this woman and I immediately thought (more of a sudden insight than a thought, really) that what had happened to this woman was a shift of consciousness from the left brain or *not-self* to the right brain or *self*. Her experience resonated with me because it was exactly what happened to me when I was on a Vipassana meditation retreat in England during 1999. However, I had almost 10 years of Buddhist training and philosophy to support me when the energy rose; this woman was not as fortunate.

In the past, when intense spiritual practices were undertaken, they frequently did not result in triggering profound spiritual experiences. This has changed. Today, intense meditation like Goenka can be done relatively safely with the knowledge that the effects of energy work bear much quicker results now than before. This puts the responsibility for informing students about the dormant energy and its effects on the teachers of spiritual practices to make sure that students are aware of the power and risks before undertaking a given practice. Is this information given to students at their first meditation evening or yoga class? I don't think so. Pity, because students need to be prepared.

The spiritual path is not a path for the fearful. When Kundalini rises in those whose approach is tentative, the result is often fear and confusion. The shift that lies in store for the practitioner must be put in a lifestyle context if it's to have a chance of not overwhelming or terrifying practitioners.

How did I learn about the emotional and psychic shocks associated with raising Kundalini? In the laboratory of my own body, of course. My conclusions are based on a combination of my own experiences and intuition.

Consider that the left brain is the ego or not-Self and the right brain is the Self. Kundalini creates a shift from left to right and then acts to bring left and right into balance. If the student knows this, he or she then realizes the energy evolves in power and form. It needs to be cooperated with, not resisted or fought against.

Having a context in which to put spiritual experience is very important to understanding, accepting, and co-operating with the process, as well as to allowing the energy to do its healing and transformative work. Without this context, spiritual practice can be a bewildering, scary experience that happens unexpectedly without the subject even being aware this energy exists, much less how its arousal can change the Being — physically, mentally, and spiritually in the weeks and months and, indeed, the years ahead.

If practitioners use the shift of consciousness from the left to the right as a model for understanding the "benign intentions" of the Kundalini energy, it will permit them to allay their fears and celebrate the moment of shifting consciousness.

I spoke to the woman. What troubled her most was having her experience validated. I told her I had a positive feeling about her experience. The advice I gave her was to stay quiet as much as she could. To continue doing everything that she had given her word to do. Since she was a student, I advised her to continue with her studies when all she wanted to do was drop out and rest. Because of the shift of consciousness, there is a huge temptation to get absorbed and fascinated by the effects of expanded consciousness. It takes great strength to ignore these and to continue doing what one gave one's word to do. Speaking about my own case, it is very important not to get taken over by such experiences, whether they be in the form of lofty ideas, blissful feelings, powerful emotions, visions, etc. All of this must be watched impassively and without attachment.

The woman was relieved when I said this as many people had been telling her that she needed to rest. I don't agree with this advice. The upsurge of energy affects the nervous system and I found that I needed to do a lot of physical exercise, so I did intensive indoor cycling to relieve the pressure. In my reading of people who have gone through similar experiences, most say that they had to do some demanding physical exercise to keep grounded and relieve the build-up of the energy. Even today, if I leave it too long without going to the gym, I begin to feel restless and irritated.

She was relieved to have her experience validated as normal and not a sign that she was "going mad"! I didn't get diverted by accounts of the various experiences she was having, both physical and mental. I didn't engage with the drama, and I think she was a little disappointed by my taking that approach. Looking back, I understand the power and pull of such experiences, but they are not IT — they are just aberrations in the nervous system caused by the awakening energy, and I don't encourage anyone to get stuck there. She is no different.

KUNDALINI AND WHITE TANTRA YOGA

"My study and practice of Mahayana Buddhism was motivated solely by my love of the Buddha and everything he said. I had no idea that there was anything beyond this on the spiritual path."

~ Author

On Saturday, I attended a day of White Tantra yoga. As a teacher of Kundalini yoga, continuing professional development is required by the Kundalini Yoga Teachers Association. Completing this day gives me 10 CEU points. I last attended this day two years ago when I began Kundalini yoga training. I had never seen myself as a yoga teacher, but activating Kundalini changed that.

My study and practice of Mahayana Buddhism was motivated solely by my love of the Buddha and everything he said. I had no idea that there was anything beyond this on the spiritual path. So, when the Kundalini energy rose during a meditation retreat, I experienced the bliss of the ignorant in that I had no idea what had happened because my mind had no label for it. I was happy enjoying its effects.

Then, one day I found a book, opened the pages, and read about this energy called Kundalini. Ah...now the mind had a label and it went to work producing all kinds of thoughts about being special and having experienced something uncommon. I came out of this ego inflation much humbler, said to myself if I have experienced it, then it makes sense that I should teach it and so, I became a Kundalini yoga teacher.

While studying and practicing Mahayana Buddhism, I always struggled with meditation. The duration of each sitting seemed so long. I preferred the practice of mindfulness. I didn't have a label for that at the time either, but being aware of everything that went on within me at all times was a process I discovered on my own through intuition. As for formal meditation, to be totally honest, I have always struggled with it and still do.

The first White Tantra Yoga day I attended two years ago, with its 31- and 62-minute meditations, was a nightmare. I was stressed from beginning to end. It was such a shock to my mind, I wound up at McDonalds eating a fishburger (I still ate fish then), chips, and a milkshake. The following year, I didn't attend this session because the memory — of how awful it was — was still fresh. This year I reasoned that since I had been teaching for almost two years, getting up and doing my own practice — including meditation — maybe I would be okay if I attended again. So I registered, not very happy about it, but feeling compelled.

I arrived early on Saturday morning and soon the sea of white that are Kundalini yoga teachers and practitioners began to form. I sat at a table looking at happy and friendly faces, wondering to myself what is was that makes me so uncomfortable around yoga devotees, at the same time I feel so committed to Kundalini because I have experienced it. Something just didn't feel right. We started the day with a 31-minute meditation. The aim of White Tantra is to dissolve/transform blocks in the subconscious. The meditation can only be done under the supervision of the Mahan Tantric, who was beamed in by video over a huge screen, giving instructions on how to do the meditation.

During these meditation sessions, I battled with my mind about the usefulness of what I was doing. Anyway, I participated fully in every session and to my relief, there was only one 62-minute meditation, during which my focus scattered.

I completed the day happy and relieved, without going to McDonalds. Since then, I've felt restless without knowing why. I haven't been able to get up and do my early morning *sadhana* which, until this day, I looked forward to.

This morning I was thinking about why. The word "responsibility" came to me. The spiritual path requires taking responsibility for every area of life. In the transformative self-development training I've done, I reviewed events, during which, past decisions I'd made either limited my possibilities or caused me trauma, which up to that point, I had refused to acknowledge. The act of examining these events and the decisions I made freed the unconscious energy so it could be transformed. It takes consciousness to be responsible.

And this is the dilemma I face about any practice that claims to clear subconscious blocks. How can they be cleared if responsibility is not taken? I was never good at accepting things on faith; I need to know for myself how transformation and its by-product, the expansion of consciousness, happen. It's not enough just to tell me that attending this day and participating in the meditation sessions suffices.

From my own experience, I know that it is only when I face up to myself and stop running away — which first occurred after Kundalini rose — that I take the responsibility not to make either myself or others appear wrong, but in just being aware that my consciousness has shifted and expanded.

Once again, I was faced with a familiar dilemma: namely, accepting what I had been told versus what I experienced. And the two couldn't possibly be more different.

KUNDALINI RISES: REVELATION OR REALIZATION?

For sure, there is revelation when Kundalini rises because there is the direct experience of the energy, which, for me, was a complete revelation, as I had no idea this energy resided within me.

~ Author

A few days ago, I found myself thinking about whether or not revelation and realization are the same; I assert they are not. Revelation is defined as "a surprising and previously unknown fact, especially one that is made known in a dramatic way." Realization, on the other hand, is defined as "the act of becoming fully aware of something as fact." Revelation may point to a realization, but is not *it*.

Revelation is like the *Aha* or *Eureka* moment which many great scientists have experienced; but, such revelation, whilst giving rise to new ways of doing things — as natural laws are revealed — hasn't, to my knowledge, resulted in the realization of the condition that underpins the revelation. Realization produces a state change in consciousness that is permanent and results in Sat, Chit, Ananda (joy, consciousness, bliss) as explained by those who have realized *Maya*. Realization is more of an *Aah*...as if it is familiar in some way.

For sure, there is revelation when Kundalini rises because there is the direct experience of the energy, which, for me, was a complete revelation, as I had no idea this energy resided within me. But whether this deepens/transforms into becoming a realization that permanently alters consciousness depends on many factors. I assert that the practice of being mindful is critical following a Kundalini awakening. Continuous mindfulness or pondering on deep spiritual questions (for example, the Zen system of koans) is mandatory in bringing about a shift of consciousness leading to realization.

Another way that revelation and realization are different is in the experiences each brings about. Revelation is often accompanied by an excitement, a seeing of something new, and a burning desire to tell everyone what has been revealed. Realization is an altogether more quiet affair, a kind of slipping into a state, a sense of contentment, a coming home.

As more Kundalini effects show up over time, it's important to take snapshots. What's happening now! You will see how the NOW changes: some effects being amplified, others disappearing, new ones coming to the fore — the never-ending march of consciousness, as it shifts from the left to the right brain, the Conscious Spirit to the Primal Spirit.

Closely tied to realization and revelation is intuition which could be said to play a part in stimulating both.

Intuition, often referred to as "the still, small voice," is our inner teacher, hence, in-*tuition*. The strength of intuition depends on the strength of consciousness and as Kundalini is the direct vehicle for expanding our grasp of consciousness, it follows that Kundalini is inextricably linked with intuition, which may be thought of as signals emanating from our subconscious to conscious minds.

Before my Kundalini rose, my intuition was very much mixed in with feelings and emotions. I would get the urge to "do something," but frequently didn't do it if I didn't feel like it.

This kind of intuition originates from the second Chakra, which is why it's not pure, untainted intuition. As Kundalini rises, the expansion of consciousness results in intuition emerging at the level of the sixth Chakra, where it is independent of feelings and/or emotions. Intuition at the sixth Chakra is more instructional, if that makes sense. I'm not saying that intuition at the sixth Chakra is better than the second variety, but only that it lends a different quality to intuition.

Before Kundalini, the still, small voice is very quiet. Acting upon it comes with a crossing of the fingers and a silent plea for things to work out. Intuition is part of the language of the soul, as is the mind with its thoughts that tend to dominate until the individual cultivates the ability to be still and listen for the still, small voice. Gradually, with enough trust, intuition expands; but, in the early stages, of the spiritual quest, it is not strong.

Kundalini meditation is one way of accessing intuition. Its purpose is to quiet the mind. As it becomes stilled, one cultivates intuition. Be aware, however, that the mind has no interest in being still or reigning in its never-ending supply of thoughts. It takes intention, as well as trust to nurture the shoots of intuition. Whenever I trusted my intuition, and acted on it, it worked — but only since Kundalini awakened.

Working with intuition opens an important point of entry into the language of the soul. After intuition comes insight, incubation, and finally, illumination when the glory of the Soul stands revealed.

THE SHIFT FROM KNOWLEDGE TO EXPERIENCE

"I have limitless compassion for these gurus because I don't think that they set out to deliberately mislead. What I do find completely unacceptable is when they still claim to have experiences which they haven't had and which it is obvious they haven't had as soon as they open their mouths."
~ Author

Recently, I commented on a certain famous guru who has made claims about Kundalini he couldn't possibly make if he had actually experienced Kundalini. After commenting, I went to my kitchen and was looking out of the window when the words of my Kundalini yoga teacher came to me: "Understand with compassion; otherwise, you will misunderstand the times."

What do these words mean?

After pondering a while, I think they underline the fact that spirituality in the Piscean Age was about accumulating knowledge and understanding spiritual writings. So many gurus learned this literature and used its theories to inspire the people who sat at their feet. They knew what the mystics and saints had written. The emphasis was on knowledge and knowing in the Piscean Age, what I call left-brain consciousness. There wasn't that much emphasis on experience.

Now we are in the Aquarian Age where seekers tend to express their spiritual longings thusly: "I know I want to experience and I want to experience from someone who has experienced, not someone who simply knows." This desire for experience is a function of a shift of consciousness from the left to the right side of the brain.

I have limitless compassion for these gurus because I don't think that they set out to deliberately mislead. What I do find completely unacceptable is when they still claim to have experiences, which they haven't had, a detail that becomes obvious as soon as they open their mouths.

My feeling is that this Aquarian Age is going to demand a level of honesty and authenticity unprecedented in the last age — not just in spirituality but in every area of life. We are moving towards being more authentic and I, for one, welcome it.

KNOW YOURSELF

"Someone who is awakened doesn't have to deal with this early stage of spiritual awakening. But each one of us, who desires to awaken, must take on this responsibility."
~ Author

A while ago, I replayed a broadcast interview given by Adyashanti, whose teaching is everywhere on the Web at the moment. I had a personal interest because prior to the program, I had sent him an email question and, like anybody who does something like this, I was eager to get an answer. With the time difference, it was too late to wait up for it, so as soon as it was available I downloaded it.

In the talk he gave before answering emails and taking calls, he spoke about two different kinds of awakenings. Given my interest in Kundalini energy, what interested me was his not speaking about Kundalini specifically, but allegorically using the incident in the Bible when Jesus was baptized and the spirit descended on him like a dove. He said that he had that kind of experience many years ago, but hadn't thought very much about it at the time. He talked about this "spirit" operating in two ways:

- The first being upward and outward, which results in a transcendent state of consciousness, a moving out of the body/mind; and
- The second, going down and in, which he says leads one to realize there is nothing wrong with the world or anything in it.

He offered the suggestion that from an early age, we are taught or decide that there is something wrong with the world; but, with this inward, deepening of the descending spirit, there is the realization that everything is exactly the way it is meant to be, and there is nothing wrong. I found this really interesting and it resonated with the two experiences I've had with this energy, which I call Kundalini solely because it was the first available label I found for it.

When his talk concluded, he went to the emails and I held my breath! He asked that the emails/phone call-ins relate to his talk.

However, the first email had to do with an unresolved issue in the writer's personal life. I listened to him go through it with a growing sense of frustration that he was moving away from the content of the talk he had just given. Then, he went to the phone to take a call and my frustration increased as he dealt with the caller's personal issues once again. While he didn't refer to my email or reference me, there were some sentences in his talk which were taken word for word from my email, so while I don't know for sure if he was influenced by my email, I was happy with the content in his main talk.

After the broadcast finished, I began to ponder. There is no doubt that without doing the work to resolve personal issues of the kind aired by the emails and call-ins, spiritual awakening is not possible.

The first commandment of spiritual awakening is "know yourself." It's the one most people want to avoid. Even after being on a spiritual path for many years, namely my involvement with Buddhism, it was only after Kundalini rose that I was forced to face the personal issues I had been running away from by hiding in the spiritual.

Someone who is awakened doesn't have to deal with this early stage of spiritual awakening. But each one of us, who desires to awaken, must take on this responsibility. There is a great danger on the spiritual path, especially for those practicing meditation and yoga, to believe that the practice itself can correct the root issues that prevent us from awakening. These can only be resolved at a conscious level when we are willing to take responsibility and stop blaming circumstances.

So, before any spiritual work is attempted, I strongly recommend individuals — especially those who have been on a spiritual path for many years — do a transformative, self-development program. In my case, it was the Forum from Landmark Worldwide, but there are others. It's not important which one is chosen. What is critical is dealing with sloppy thinking that says: simply by meditating or doing yoga, one is able to subdue the ego.

No matter how spiritually advanced one might consider oneself to be, one must ask, "Is there something hidden from me that, were it to be revealed, would change everything?" The ego has no interest in this question. But when you think about it, knowing yourself is but a small price to pay for awakening. Not only is it essential to awakening, it is also a forward step in self-realization.

Other Titles by Life Force Books

Deciphering the Golden Flower One Secret at a Time
JJ Semple - Life Force Books, *2007*

A clinical study of the author's spiritual development process, this book describes how he used *The Secret of the Golden Flower* to awaken his Kundalini and reverse the effects of a childhood accident.

The Backward-Flowing Method: The Secret of Life and Death
JJ Semple - Life Force Books, *2008*

For the first time ever, a book dares to reveal the secrets of the world's most influential meditation method – a series of techniques originally compiled in the 9th. Century masterpiece of Chinese alchemy, *The Secret of the Golden Flower*. One-by-one, the author reveals the techniques behind these meditation secrets, providing clear instructions on how to use them.

The Biology of Consciousness: Case Studies in Kundalini
JJ Semple - Life Force Books, *2014*

Kirkus Reviews had this to say: "The author fleshes out the book with a dramatic section devoted to case studies of different types of Kundalini encounters, showing the different ways that practitioners "awaken" energies inside themselves, as well as how Kundalini helps people tackle personal challenges. These studies give the work an instantly relatable, human dimension that's often missing from books of this kind and underscores Semple's approachable, ordinary-guy tone throughout. New readers approaching this complicated subject will feel immediately at ease, and longtime Kundalini practitioners will no doubt find details that remind them of their own experiences."

Available on Amazon, online stores, and at bookstores throughout the world, in Print and eBook formats.